Red Rag
TO A
Bull!

Red Rag TO A Bull!

DR MAGNUS PYKE'S DICTIONARY OF FALLACIES

WILLOW BOOKS
Collins
8 Grafton Street, London
1983

Willow Books
William Collins Sons & Co Ltd
London . Glasgow . Sydney . Auckland
Toronto . Johannesburg

First published in Great Britain 1983
© Magnus Pyke 1983

Cartoons by Graham Thompson

Pyke, Magnus
Red rag to a bull!
1. Curiosities and wonders
I. Title
001.9   AG243

ISBN 0 00 218016 2

Filmset by Ace Filmsetting Ltd, Frome
Printed in Great Britain by
William Collins Sons & Co, Glasgow

CONTENTS

PROLOGUE

It could be thought a matter of little importance to believe what I was taught when I was a child, that picking the shell off a boiled egg would cause warts to grow on my fingers. Now that I am a grown man, however, I *do* think that it is a serious matter to believe in fallacies, even little ones. That is the reason why I have written this book. Today, the fallacy may concern nothing more than warts, the good luck following the sighting of a black cat or the bad luck coming from walking under a ladder: but tomorrow it may be something much more important, perhaps the bankruptcy of a business whose owner bought a half-million-pound computer he did not need because he believed his horoscope on the back page of the morning paper when it told him that 'today is the day to take bold financial decisions'. Most horrible of all was the fallacy of the Aryan master race which told its believers that they were justified in exterminating millions of their fellow men.

There are fallacies, of course, which are little more than quaint mistakes. There are those who fallaciously convince themselves that a medicine described as a 'carminative' is one that makes you calm – a tranquillizer, in fact. 'Carminative' actually means, as is primly described in the dictionary, 'having the quality of expelling wind'. Other fallacies are bigger and more important mistakes, based on people believing what they have always believed or, as in the fallacy of *my* country, or town, or regiment, or football club, is the best in the world, in their believing what they want to believe.

There are numerous records of tribes, some primitive but some not so primitive who, indeed, consider themselves advanced and civilized, indulging in rain dances designed to affect the weather. This leads us to a fine crop of fallacies based on beliefs often handed down from the past and accepted as gospel. It is not all that long since it was generally accepted that castor oil, a powerful and disagreeable laxative, was a cure for virtually every ill from acne to scarlet fever. This fallacy dated back to the early centuries of medical practice. Even today, in this so-called age of scientific thinking, it is easy for people to slide into beliefs for which there is very little rational foundation. For example, much of the talk about how healthy people were in the good old days is a fallacy. In fact, the good old days were not healthy at all. For a start, people did not live as long as they do now but died of cholera, smallpox, plague and even the ague (which was malaria). They did not survive long enough to contract the so-called 'diseases of civilization' from which – because we have to die of *something* – we die today. Nor need I concern myself here with such up-to-date fallacies as un-identified flying objects (UFOs) and the little men with protruding green eyes they bring with them, the Loch Ness Monster, spoon-bending, pyramidology, and the determination of the sex of an unborn child by the swing of a wedding ring suspended on a hair over the mother's abdomen. Some of these are dealt with later on.

Part of the dignity and greatness of man and woman is based on reason. 'He that made us', wrote Shakespeare, 'gave us not that god-like reason to fust in us unused'. And again he wrote, 'What a piece of work is a man. How noble in reason! How infinite in faculty!' What we are and what we have become, our understanding of the universe, our ability to fly to the moon, to heal the sick (or at least more of them than our ancestors could), to see what is going on a thousand miles away – our scientific achievements – have all come from the use of reason. On the contrary, I believe that when we fall a slave to unreason, that is to fallacy, we disgrace ourselves. That is why I want to make it clear, even though I am sure you already know it in your heart, that throwing spilt salt over your left shoulder will not affect your future prosperity a bit. It is a fallacy to imagine otherwise.

ASTROLOGY

The continued belief, at a trivial level, in astrology is one of the most remarkable aberrations of the modern age. The notion that the position of the stars and planets, the sun and the moon, at the exact hour and date of one's birth has anything to do with one's subsequent career is a fallacy so blatant that it is hard to imagine that anyone would give credence to such rubbish. This is quite apart from the fact that the poet Dean Swift gave the death blow in the minds of any thinking person to such residual credence in astrology as existed in his day – and that was three hundred years ago. Yet we still find popular newspapers with circulations in the millions devoting daily a significant number of their expensive column-inches to astrology, under such headings as *Your Stars, Startime* or *What the stars foretell.* Nor would hard-headed newspaper proprietors persist in publishing such stuff if there were not readers sufficiently simple and misguided to read it.

'Of course', a friend will tell you, with a self-conscious giggle, 'although I do read the astrology section in the paper – I'm a Scorpio myself, you know – I don't really believe it. But you'd be surprised how often what they print is right.'

It could be argued that even though the crowning achievement of the human race has been the use of reason and that, mainly within the last century of human history, the use of reason as exemplified by science has enabled us to master infectious disease, to fly, to light our houses with electricity and, latest of all, to convey music, drama, poetry, news and sport by television, there is no harm in the astrology pages in the daily papers; they merely amuse. I disagree. I believe that there is harm. The table which follows, giving side by side the very different prophecies of four different newspapers all for the same day, 12 August 1982, demonstrates the triviality of the nonsense laid out for the gullible reader. Should it be argued that this is merely a bit of fun, why then, I ask, is it presented as if it should be taken seriously? More important, however, is the blunting effect on the mind of pretending, even in play, that one's birthday, assigning an individual to Sagittarius or Pisces, to Gemini or Virgo, can exert any effect, good or bad, on one's behaviour, character or fortune in life.

It does no harm to one's health, the medical scientists may report, to bemuse one's senses by smoking cannabis. Even though this may be true, it is generally agreed that a society – or an individual – aiming for great achievement, is well advised to avoid indulgence in cannabis. I would equally advise avoidance of fallacy if one wishes to retain a clear mind and particularly of a fallacy which pretends to deal in astrological prophecies, most particularly of all when they are wrapped up in the ambiguous all-things-to-all-men prose of daily journalism.

Because the ancient Babylonians believed that the fate and future of human beings could be forecast from the position of the stars, there is no reason why we should do so now. As it happens, the Babylonian priests had two ways for ascertaining the will and intention of the gods. One was astrology, the other hepatoscopy. This involved the inspection of the liver of sacrificial animals. After an animal has been slaughtered, its liver is full of blood. It was, therefore, thought that the liver must be the seat of the soul. It soon came to be believed that the shape, the size and the markings of the liver indicated what the gods had in mind for the man who had donated it to the temple. It would, therefore, be no more irrational for the daily papers to pretend to deduce the future happiness or the success in love or in getting on with their bosses of their readers from the scrutiny of the livers of the lambs, pigs and oxen of the animals providing their Sunday joints as from their birthdays.

Once upon a time, one might suppose that there could have been a certain twisted logic in using the date and time of birth as the starting point for drawing up a person's horoscope, even though some soothsayers made their computations from the position of the sun, moon and stars at the time of conception, nine months before birth. But today the use of such hocus-pocus, whether linked to conception or birth, seems completely dotty in view of the fact that there is no serious problem in virtually selecting a date for a baby's birth by inducing it almost at will. Are we seriously to concern ourselves, even if we *do* read a popular paper employing an astrolo-

	EXPRESS	MAIL	MIRROR	SUN
Aquarius *Jan 21 Feb 19*	Maintain a low profile at work as assertive tactics could meet with a rebuff from people in higher authority.	A helpful day for working relationships but not such encouraging trends domestically. Money matters could give rise to friction, but avoid arguments. If equipment needs servicing, see to it now.	You could be taking up a sport or hobby that will make you new friends.	You will encourage youngsters to strike out on their own. There could be a worry, though. It might concern an unexpected bill.
Pisces *Feb 20 Mar 20*	Do your best to clear up unfinished work. You will make little headway with new jobs. Caution to both motorists and pedestrians; keep road safety rules in mind.	Financial prospects are improving and mixing business with pleasure will pay off late in the day. This morning check details of contracts and other agreements. Don't sell yourself short. Allow for odd discrepancy or misunderstanding.	Others may try to influence you but only you know what you really want. A car journey may be planned.	Good day for making money. A talk with a bank manager will be particularly helpful. You have the ability to bargain at the moment. All is well at home, with the family at peace with itself. You could be forgetful at work.
Aries *Mar 21 Apr 20*	Take care that what's been well organized doesn't go awry. Resist the urge to make changes in arrangements. If taking part in sport, guard against mishaps; same applies if handling machinery.	Unlikely you'll get through all you've set yourself so sort out the essentials. Allow time for the lighter side of life and include friendly contact with people who can help you push ahead. Avoid business dealings at lunch.	People you know could be influential. Don't be afraid to ask for help. A plane trip is possible.	You are in a restless mood and hate being cooped up somewhere boring. A service could be withdrawn for a while. Travelling will cost more than you expect. There is a lot of fun on your holidays.

	EXPRESS	MAIL	MIRROR	SUN
Taurus *Apr 21 May 21*	If you're faced with problems today, they are likely to be domestic. Elsewhere you'll accomplish more on your own than with the help of others.	Keep your mind on the main points if you are contemplating changes at home or at work and don't be influenced by damping comments this morning. In general, look for economy in time, energy and money.	Be careful of losing something. Make sure you are insured. Buying someone a gift could be appreciated.	You could have trouble in coming up with the right answers. You must try to pay your own way. If you owe money make a clear promise to pay. There's competition in your life but your heart's not in it.
Gemini *May 22 Jun 21*	No escape from pressure of work. Arrangements made with relatives might suffer a setback. Family matters seem aggravating but keep grievances to yourself.	You may be torn between the old and the new but it is probably time to think about updating your ideas in line with changing patterns. However don't rock the boat today. Adjustments must be well thought out.	There may be some sadness around you and you will be trying to sort out things in a sensible way. Events happen rather quickly.	A better day with a bit of luck to cheer you on your way. Be prepared to spend the evening with friends with a few surprises along the way. Lucky colour – blue.
Cancer *Jun 22 Jul 23*	You may be tempted to see more of friends but there are financial obstacles. You may suffer a disappointment if you are hoping for business opportunities through friends.	News on the way about a close companion and changes which occur should benefit your own prospects. If socializing at lunch time be prepared to spend more than you anticipate and try not to be left holding the bag.	Talk about education, schools and children is likely. You could be decorating or improving your home. It's a rather busy and expensive time but worth it.	If someone is trying to sell you something, back off and think about it. An uncle or aunt could give you some good advice. Good time for romance.

	EXPRESS	MAIL	MIRROR	SUN
Leo *Jul 24* *Aug 23*	You may be forced to go along with people at work who are rearranging things, but don't be tempted to make any changes yourself. A mistake to try to move a step higher up the ladder of success – you'd be mistaking your approach to people in power.	Morning news could mean a rearrangement of the day's programme but try not to chop and change without good reason. People in positions of authority might stir up minor irritations this morning. Don't be upset.	A person who is behaving badly or deceitfully makes you feel fed up. A big decision is necessary soon. Tax matters could need your attention.	There could be a special link with the armed services in some way. There could be restless nights if you have a problem on your mind. Industrial action could affect the delivery of something you are anxious to have.
Virgo *Aug 24* *Sep 23*	Curb impatience to speed the outcome of what you're planning. Day when you may be subjected to aggravation regarding travel. It will be anything but a pleasure now.	Allow plenty of time for morning journeys. Communication could be a problem first half of the day, and you might waste time on fruitless visits and meetings. The afternoon is better for getting around.	This is a happy and lucky time. Lots of fun is indicated and overseas travel is well starred.	A cheerful day when your personality is at its brightest. Your regular partner will find you good company. You will get on well with someone new. Be cautious about buying something expensive.
Libra *Sep 24* *Oct 23*	Others could be wasting resources you have put at their disposal. Make it clear that if expenses are to be pooled, you're not prepared to pay more than your fair share.	Business matters are on your mind, but there won't be much incentive to push ahead today. A ticking-over period so far as adventurous projects are concerned. So skim through routine work and tie up loose ends.	Be patient with someone close to you who is unhappy or unsettled. Be firm but kind. Arguments occur which make you feel under a strain.	You may be uneasy about someone's behaviour, but you should be prepared to give him or her the benefit of the doubt.

	EXPRESS	MAIL	MIRROR	SUN
Scorpio *Oct 24 Nov 22*	You may feel that others are ganging up on you or taking advantage of your good nature. It is time to let them know you won't stand for it. Be cautious about decisions about legal matters.	Rivals will be active this morning but you have the advantage in competitive areas and need not be too affected by problems around the middle of the day. Keep out of trivial arguments with associates.	Listening to music or doing some creative work will help you relax. Be careful about your health.	There's a nice influence today encouraging you to look over the horizon. If you're travelling, you'll have a lovely time. If involved in sport, there could be a hold up. Romance looks promising, so look good.
Sagittarius *Nov 23 Dec 22*	On the surface, relationships with colleagues may seem peaceful; but don't take it for granted. Make sure you give them no reason for ill-will.	An edgy morning if you let yourself be too influenced by restless conditions. Try not to get caught up in time-wasting trivialities. The second half of the day is best for all activities.	A meeting this week could be important. Some pointed questions may be asked.	You get on well with Libran and Capricorn folk today. Tell the truth – there is nothing to be frightened of. Be on the lookout for an unusual happening. Lucky number: 4.
Capricorn *Dec 23 Jan 20*	Steer clear of social surroundings now. Meetings with friends are likely to result in tension. If in love, be on guard against a rival for your partner's affections.	There may be some difficulty in organizing a group activity this morning. Associates will be intent on their own affairs, so don't count on easy co-operation. Check every social arrangement before setting out.	You may need to take an animal to the vet or you could be booking up kennels. A decision is necessary about your love life.	You start thinking about the past, trying to find guidance about the future. Religion could be much in your thoughts. At work someone may be cheating a little, which makes you unhappy. At home there is a cosy air.

gist, that the new-born General Secretary of the Union, who seemed so safely heading towards being a Cancer with a birthday on 23 June, had instead to put up with the status of a Gemini for the whole of his life because the doctor induced his birth a week early?

The regular movements of the sun, the moon and the planets appeared to the Babylonians and, three thousand years or so later, to the Greeks, to signify the rule of law in the heavens. In contrast, the life of man was unruly and at the caprice of storm and tempest, earthquake and disaster, war and pillage. It was, therefore, excusable for them, if not for us, with our accumulation of another three thousand years of experience, demonstrating the fallacy of the whole idea, to try to link the movements of the heavenly bodies with the behaviour of men and women on earth.

There is cause for shame at the members of a modern community, which can rightly claim to be advanced in civilization, knowledge and science, who believe – or even half-believe – that because they were born between 21 April and 21 May they belong to the constellation of Taurus and are therefore different from their neighbour born on 1 August, who consequently owes tribute to the constellation of Leo. Even in fun, it is surely puerile to be told by *The Sun* newspaper, of all authorities, that because you were born between 23 November and 22 December your lucky number is 4 and you should not be afraid to speak the truth on Thursday. On the other hand, had you been born during the first fortnight of March, 12 August 1982 was a good day to make money (presumably whether you spoke the truth or not). What is pitiful about this, is that the modern astrologers have clung to the basic fallacy of astrology, which is the delusion that the movements of astronomical bodies influence human behaviour and foretell the fate of one particular individual, even to forecasting whether he is to have a disagreement with his employer.

Yet during the long history of astrology, some good did come from it. In mapping the skies for the fruitless purpose of casting a horoscope, the astrologers gradually learned more and more about the movements of the moon, the planets and the stars until, as the centuries passed, this part of their knowledge was gradually converted into the science of astronomy. How much better it would have been had the multitude of readers of popular papers turned their minds to the remarkable new findings of astronomy and let the superstitious fallacies of our distant ancestors lie forgotten in the limbo they deserve. After all, we don't believe any more that it is the moon that makes a man a lunatic, that a saturnine person got that way because of the influence of Saturn (but see Moon – effect on human behaviour), or that it was the stars that really made our plans go wrong when we call them ill-starred. These are the last residues of astrology. Don't let us add to them.

B

BALDNESS

'To cure baldness', wrote John Wesley in a little book he brought out in 1747, to reinforce his ministry of prayer with the art of healing, 'rub the part morning and evening with *onions* until it is red; and rub it afterwards with *honey*'. Should this treatment be

ineffective, he had another. 'Wash [the part] with a decoction of boxwood: tried.' And even if this tried remedy should prove unsuccessful, Wesley had a third: 'Electrify it daily.'

Unfortunately, all three of Wesley's eighteenth century treatments were fallacious. But then so was that included, perhaps unwisely, in the 1956 edition of the *Encyclopaedia Britannica*, where it is claimed that 'though (baldness) progresses steadily if neglected, (it) is very amenable to treatment by sulphur and salicylic acid, 18gr of each added to one ounce of vaseline . . . This should be rubbed well into the scalp daily for a prolonged period.' But then, purported cures for baldness are legion, which is one further indication of the persistence with which people cling to those fallacies which they *wish* were true but which, in their hearts, they know to be false – in this instance because of the number of bald men to be seen.

There are several reasons why it is not altogether easy to think clearly about baldness. For a start, there are several forms of baldness. It can, for example, start at the back of the head, like a monk's tonsure. Or it can creep up the parting. Some men go bald in their twenties, others become 'thin on top' and only go bald when they are old. The evidence, however, is strong that a susceptibility to baldness is inherited, although whether it is due to one gene or to several is less clear. An added complication is sex. Aristotle was not quite right when he wrote: 'No boy ever gets bald, no woman and no castrated man.' Women *can* become bald and so can eunuchs, but the numbers of either who do are very few – as the genes for baldness do not operate if the concentration of androgens (male hormones) is low. A further complication is that the hair does tend to become sparse for both men and women as old age advances. What, however, is perfectly clear is that the idea that the multitude of so-called remedies and preventatives offered by hopeful manufacturers is going to do any good is a fallacy.

Baldness is predominantly restricted to men and is genetically controlled. If a young lady is hesitant about marrying a young gentleman for fear that he should go bald in later life, she should investigate the heads of his brothers, his father, his uncles and his grandfathers. If many of them are, or were, bald, the likelihood is that he will go bald too, and there is also a good chance that among her sons, some will grow up to become bald men. There is only one virtually certain remedy to prevent a genetically susceptible young man developing a bald head or, if his baldness is already beginning, to stop it. Castration halts the production of male hormones and is almost always a cure. This remedy, however, would be of little help to the doubtful girlfriend.

BERMUDA TRIANGLE

In times past, when people were ignorant of the rational workings of the remarkable world in which we live, there was some excuse for their believing in the existence of fabulous monsters and undiscovered lands where a man and his ship might be carried off – up into the sky or down to the bottom of the sea – never to be heard of again. Today, knowledge of the earth and the creatures in it (much of which is due to modern science, which has led to an explosion of understanding unprecedented in history virtually within a generation), tells us that mermaids, ogres and dragons are figments of uneducated imagination.

The so-called 'Bermuda Triangle' is an ill-defined area of ocean extending roughly from Bermuda to the southern tip of Florida, the Bahamas and Puerto Rica. In the early days of the Spanish incursions into America, this area, at that time incompletely charted, was dangerous to the navigators of sailing ships. It earned, in consequence, an unsavoury reputation and was justifiably feared by voyagers. The current unfortunate interest in the Bermuda Triangle was stimulated by a book written by Charles Berlitz, of which several million copies were sold in the United States and elsewhere. Whether intentionally or by inadvertence, this book battened on to all the latent unreason and credulity of the present age. The implication of Berlitz's narrative was that malevolent supernatural forces existed within the Bermuda Triangle whereby modern ships and aircraft were spirited away to disappear without trace, never to be seen again. The book purported to describe, with full supporting detail, the inexplicable disappearance of a squadron of aircraft from the US Navy base at Fort Lauderdale, the vanishing of a depressing roll of ships, and much more. As with alleged reports of unidentified flying objects, once the respectability of print had been given to such extra-terrestrial happenings, reports poured in from credulous people eager to be terrified by the occult. By 1973, the Arizona State University was able to publish a comprehensive bibliography of such supernatural goings-on.

When, however, it is possible to examine with care the evidence purporting to support the existence of dark satanic forces, sucking down to their doom ships, planes and men, it becomes clear that the whole business is a fallacy. The American bombers, navigated by trainee pilots, were lost, as other pilots have been lost before. The rescue aircraft was seen to explode before dropping into the sea. Careful study by Graham Massey in 1976 and in the *New Scientist* in 1977, both of the facts themselves and of the descriptions given by Berlitz and his followers, failed to support any suggestion that the paranormal was involved in what happened in the Bermuda Triangle or in other areas of the sea in which similar occult incidents have been claimed to have occurred.

BLACK CATS

It is a fallacy to believe that the possession of a cat, whether black or any other colour, brings good luck, or that the sight of a black cat running across the road in front of a person, has any influence, good or bad, on his subsequent wellbeing. In short, the idea that black cats bring good luck is nonsense. The idea that it is the blackness of the cat which gives it this fictitious potency is mainly restricted to Great Britain. In the United States, Belgium and Spain, so far as the superstition holds sway at all, it is generally believed that it is white cats which are lucky.

Cats, it seems, were first domesticated in Egypt in about 3000 BC and were put to work catching mice in granaries and food stores.

Their usefulness led to their being put under the protection of one of the gods. In later classical times they were transferred to Diana. It could be argued that the attribution of some measure of divinity to cats, even such as the current fallacy of their bringing luck, was an indulgence of harmless sentimentality. This, however, may not be so. My argument throughout this book is that fallacies can be dangerous, even malevolent, and that a civilized society should have no dealings with them. By medieval times, cats – particularly black ones – had become associated with witches and broomsticks. And so we now see the trivial association of cats with good luck reinforcing one of the most horrible fallacies in history: the belief in witches. This blot on human behaviour, whereby harmless old women were hounded to death after being subjected to terrible acts of cruelty, shows what can arise from mindless belief in fallacy.

It has been truly said that the quality of a society can be measured by the attitude of its citizens to their domestic animals. Today there are signs that our attitude to cats (and dogs) is being changed for the worse by our attachment to another popular fallacy discussed later on (Medical Fallacies). In our laudable efforts to improve public health, the idea has grown up that we should so organize our affairs as to avoid *every* risk. Cats, therefore, should not only be forbidden to sun themselves in the window of the newsagent's shop for fear that they contaminate the toffee jars, but they should also be kept out of our domestic kitchens, and children should not be allowed to stroke them. Perhaps cats – whether black or white – are unlucky in the fallacies with which they become associated. Witchcraft was very bad, to be sure, but it is not good to believe that in this life *all* risks to health can be avoided, or that we achieve a better society if, while safeguarding our health, we withdraw our love and concern from our domestic animals. After all, not all cats have fleas.

★

BOMBAY DUCK

Bombay Duck is not duck at all. Most people make their acquaintance with it at an Indian restaurant where, if they have not been warned, they find it is what I always consider to be rather a tough, stringy, dried fish about the size of the pod of a scarlet runner. It is salted during the drying process, and consequently it has a strong salty – as well as a fishy – taste.

Why, you may ask, is it called a duck when it is actually a fish?

Part of the answer is that there is in the waters of southern Asia a small fish, the colloquial name of which, according to Englishmen returning home from India in 1673, was *bummalo*. Its proper name is actually *Harpodon nehereus*. Generations of Anglo-Indians, ordering the ambiguous fish delicacy (if you can call it such) which I have just described, and believing it to be *bummalo*, converted the name to Bombay Duck which, in fact, is really *Saurus ophiodon*.

It is undoubtedly a fallacy to believe that Bombay Duck is duck. It is equally a fallacy to describe one thing as something quite different, particularly if you want to avoid confusion.

CAESAREAN SECTION

Caesarean section, the delivery of a baby through a surgical incision in the mother's abdomen, was known in ancient medicine but was seldom performed. In the days before the existence of bacteria had been discovered and aseptic procedures in surgery developed, the chances of the mother surviving such an operation were very low. Even in the early nineteenth century, the mortality rate was 75 per cent or more. Since Caesar's mother was still alive when Caesar invaded Britain, it is virtually certain that it is a fallacy to imagine that he was born by Caesarean section. The origin of the name for this particular procedure probably arose from the Roman law, passed long before Julius Caesar's time, making it compulsory to remove premature infants from the wombs of all women who died in advanced pregnancy. This ordnance was known as the *Lex Caesaria*.

CAMEL'S HAIR BRUSH

The above item offers a wide scope for confusion, misunderstanding and error. For a start, it is unclear whether, on the face of it, it refers to an implement designed to brush the hair of a camel, that is to say to a hair brush, or whether it is intended to convey the meaning of a brush, the bristles of which are made from the hair of a camel. The whole matter, it might be claimed, could be cleared up quite simply by the use of a hyphen. This would make plain whether the word 'hair' was intended to be part of the adjective 'camel's-hair', or part of the noun 'hair-brush'. Unfortunately, a fallacy now comes in to add further to the confusion. Over the past two hundred years, it has been the practice to describe as 'camel's hair' what is, in fact, the long hairs of a squirrel's tail. This material has been used in the manufacture of fine paint-brushes used by artists.

To attribute hair to a camel when it really comes from a squirrel is not the only way in which the camel has been misused. Surely enlightenment is not enhanced by calling, as is accepted practice, an ostrich a 'camel-bird' or a specimen of the creatures known as *Mantis* a 'camel insect'. Yet this, too, is accepted usage.

But a camel's hair brush! Really!

CATGUT

In a rational world, one could hope that words would convey their meaning without ambiguity. In the real world this is not so and fallacy is rife. The strings of violins, harps and other musical instruments, as well as those of archery bows, even the strings by which the weights of clocks are sometimes suspended, and the sutures used in surgery, may all be made of catgut. And catgut is made from the entrails of sheep. Sometimes those of horses, mules and donkeys are used, but never those of cats. 'Catgut' is a corruption of 'kitgut', the string used in a 'kit', which is a sixteenth-century word for a small fiddle once popular with dancing masters.

CENTIPEDE

It is a fallacy to imagine that because a creature is called a centipede it must have a hundred feet. But although this is a fallacy, it is only a trivial one, and one from which good may come. Pick up a centipede in Great Britain and what do you find? An animal with a head possessing a pair of feelers, attached to a long segmented body, each segment of which is provided with a pair of legs. Since there are fifteen of these segments in the creatures to be found running about in fields and gardens, such members of the *Lithobiomorpha*, the common European centipede, can be seen to possess, not a hundred, but thirty feet.

Having noticed that centipedes do not necessarily possess a hundred feet, it may be that the disappointed observer will feel enough curiosity to look into the matter further. Quite soon he or she will find that centipedes are well worth attention. There are some which hatch out of their eggs already possessing all the legs and feet they are ever going to possess. Others emerge with only seven pairs of legs, giving them just fourteen feet as a start. Afterwards they go through a number of periods of growth, during each of which they change their skins and increase their number of segments, with a consequent increase in the number of feet. Some of these when full grown do come to possess very nearly a hundred legs. More remarkable still, these members of the *Geophilomorpha* can make themselves luminous underneath. This is particularly strange because they themselves are blind. Other centipedes, again, can deliver a poisonous bite sufficiently powerful to kill a man.

Centipedes are to be found world-wide and have been known from times of antiquity. Fossil centipedes from even longer ago in the Oligocene age have been identified. Compared with such fascinating truths available about so absorbing a creature, who could be other than grateful for the fallacy of its name, drawing attention to so remarkable a member of the animal kingdom?

CHEESE FOR MOUSETRAPS

It is almost universally accepted in educated societies that cheese is the favourite food of mice. The automatic choice of bait for a mousetrap is, consequently, cheese. Indeed, it is commonplace to describe the most inexpensive and undistinguished type of Cheddar cheese as 'mousetrap'. As it happens, however, mice, and rats as well, are remarkably catholic in their tastes and will eagerly consume virtually any of the food commodities eaten by people, with the possible exception of fruit and vegetables. Mice and rats are able to synthesize their requirements of vitamin C within their own bodies and consequently have no need for these two items of diet.

The fallacious nature of the belief in the particular attractiveness of cheese for rodents can readily be seen from the fact that professional exterminators do not use it. For instance, not necessarily when setting traps but when laying down poisons such as Warfarin, they attract the rats and mice with bran or other cereal offal.

The similarity of the tastes of mice and men has been strikingly demonstrated by some recent work carried out in a number of research laboratories. These studies were aimed at investigating obesity and why it is that some people readily become fat while others, often eating as much as or more than their fellows, do not. The animals were able to eat as much as they wanted of a laboratory mixture providing all their nutritional needs. Then, from time to time, they were offered as extras a whole range of 'human' foods, not cheese, mark you, but sweet cake, biscuits, paté and the like. They partook of these with enthusiasm, and while some retained their original weight, others grew fat. I refer to these studies, not from the point of view of obesity and its causes, but to illustrate the fallacy of the belief that rats and mice are especially addicted to cheese.

CHLOROPHYLL

The fallacy connecting chlorophyll and body smell that blew up, had its heyday for a few years and then died away is a splendid example of the type of unreason called by logicians *non sequitur*, to which reference is made under the heading 'Crooked Thinking'.

It was in the late 1950s that one or two minor reports appeared in medical literature on the use of poultices made out of leaves in the treatment of suppurating wounds. Among the various benefits of the treatment, the author claimed that the leaves appeared to control the smell, which is one of the more disagreeable features in the management of wound infection. He speculated that the pigment, chlorophyll, which gives leaves their green colour, might be the active agent suppressing the smell.

In the United States at that time a lot of attention was being paid, both by members of the public and by the manufacturers who served them – and their advertising agents – to personal aroma. It had come to be believed that popular acclaim and public success could only be won by those who were entirely free from body odour. Disgrace and ostracism would be the fate of anyone suffering from halitosis which, as defined by the *Oxford English Dictionary*, is abnormally foul breath. Almost as soon as the trials of leaf poultices on infected wounds had been reported, the fallacy was launched. Manufacturers of a variety of articles ranging from toothpaste to toilet paper accepted the *non sequitur* (a) that because the healing effect of the leaves was followed by the lessening of smell it was chlorophyll that did it, which was by no means established and (b) that chlorophyll prevents smells. Lack of evidence notwithstanding, the toothpaste-makers announced to the public that their brand contained chlorophyll, thus ensuring sweet breath to anyone who bought it. The soap-makers produced green tablets, guaranteed to quell body odour. Chlorophyll lozenges appeared on the market for prudent people to suck. It was even possible to buy green socks as presents for men with sweaty feet. Chlorophyll became of major commercial significance and millions of people bought chlorophyll-impregnated products. In the end it dawned on everyone that the whole thing was a fallacy. Its death knell was sounded by a satirical versifier, but only after the credulous had believed for years that, as they had known all the time –

the goat that reeks on yonder hill
has browsed all day on chlorophyll.

CHOP SUEY

When the inscrutable waiter presents you with the menu filled with upwards of sixty dishes and asks you to make your selection, you can be forgiven for that momentary wish that you'd gone to the local Berni Inn instead of trying your hand, and palate, on Chinese food. As your eyes gaze at the bewildering catalogue, one familiar name pops up and you order it with relief – 'One chop suey please'. You can't get a more Chinese dish than that, you might think: though, if you do, I'm afraid that you and the truth must part company.

The ingredients are unquestionably rich in Oriental flavour: bean sprouts, bamboo shoots, water chestnuts, rice, soy sauce, to say nothing of the tiny pieces of meat or fish. The name too is nothing if not Chinese – Cantonese if you wish to be pedantic. It means, as you might expect from the ingredients, 'mixed bits' or, more practically, 'odds and ends'. Rumour has it that this concoction was first prepared by Chinese cooks. So where lies the fallacy?

The answer is in chop suey's very conception. The masters of Oriental cuisine, ever enterprising and with an eye on a profitable market, created this 'authentic recipe' to appeal to foreign visitors, notably Americans, who presumably knew what Chinese food ought to have been like, even though the food they found in the country didn't at first quite fill the bill. Chop suey arrived and everybody was happy. Today the Chinese look on it as an agreeable *foreign* dish. As the *Rochester Post-Express* of 8 June 1904 (the earliest reference in the *Oxford English Dictionary* to the dish) tells us: 'One of the Chinese merchants of New York ... explained that chop suey is really an American dish, not known in China, but believed by Americans to be the one great national dish of the Celestials.'

So there you have it. *Bon appétit.*

COPPER BANGLES

Rheumatism is a condition associated with inflammation and pain in the joints. It is used by ordinary laymen to describe any kind of pain or stiffness, whether of the joints or muscles. In spite of advances in the science of rheumatology, what the ordinary person understands as rheumatism is a widespread and intractable condition with which doctors and their patients struggle, with greater or less success, over the years. This being so, an accumulation of folk wisdom has grown up on the subject. Some of this has a backing of good observation and truth connected, if not with the weather, at least with the climate. Sufferers in Great Britain have some reason for believing that their rheumatism will be eased if they are able to spend the winter in Egypt.

John Wesley, in his pocket book on physic published in 1747, listed the following 'cures' for rheumatism:

Cold baths.

Rub in warm treacle and apply brown paper smeared therewith.

Drink a pint of tar-water night and morning.

Drink, lying down, half a pint of white wine in which 6 or 7 cloves of garlic have been steeped.

Take 3 teaspoonfuls at night and 2 in the morning of an equal mixture of brimstone and honey.

Live on white bread and whey for a fortnight.

Take 3 or 4 times a day the quantity of a nutmet of an equal mixture of green rhubarb and lump sugar.

Since there is no hard evidence of the effectiveness of any of these treatments, it is not possible to reach certain conclusions about their usefulness. What does appear to be clear, however, is that it is a fallacy to believe in the validity of the current cult of wearing a copper bangle as a relief for rheumatism. It looks as if we shall have to go on waiting for the medical scientists.

★

CROCODILE TEARS

The notion that a crocodile sheds hypocritical tears of sorrow over the fate of the victim which it is itself tearing to pieces and devouring is another of those fallacies – like that of the ostrich burying its head in the sand, assuming it is stupid enough to imagine that because it thus cannot see, it cannot be seen, or of a bull being enraged

because the rag being waved in front of it is red – based on zoological illiteracy.

Like all other animals, a crocodile feels an emotion of satisfaction as it eats the prey it has captured. The fallacy that it is crying as it eats arises, partly, from the fact that it makes grunting and moaning noises as it eats. These sounds could be claimed to bear some resemblance to those of sobbing and crying. It also happens that when the crocodile eats, an area in the upper part of its mouth adjacent to its salivary glands causes simultaneously a flow of liquid from its eyes. It is, however, a fallacy to believe that it is crying or that it is tears that it sheds. Far from feeling sorry at what it is doing, the crocodile is pleased and is not pretending otherwise.

CROOKED THINKING

The reason why fallacies arise and people come to believe in them is because so many of us do not know how to think straight. Or, to put the matter in a more academic way, we do not grasp the principles of logic. Today, in the age of the computer, which cannot fail to be anything other than logical, we cannot afford the luxury of crooked thinking.

To the expert in logic, there are at least eight ways of misinterpreting the facts of a situation and consequently coming to a fallacious conclusion. On top of this, there are half a dozen different ways of expressing the conclusions we have reached so that they will be misunderstood when we try to explain them.

Let us start by considering the eight ways of reaching wrong conclusions from the facts themselves. These are called *material* fallacies. The first comes from confusing the accidental with the essential. For example, before refrigerators came into use, it was commonly believed that thunder made the milk go sour. Of course it was not thunder that soured the milk; the essential factor was the hot weather during which thunder-storms are most likely to occur. Then there is *secundum quid*, which is arguing from the general to the particular. It does not follow that because men wear trousers, if you're wearing trousers you're a man. Third in the logician's list is the group of fallacies based on *irrelevant conclusions*. All too often, attempts are made to prove a plaintiff is in the wrong, not by the evidence against him, but by abusing his attorney.

Begging the question is a popular approach to fallacy. 'M'lud, my client cannot possibly be guilty of stabbing his wife because everyone knows that stabbing is un-English.' Or one can use the *fallacy of the consequent*. This involves the argument that because a drunk is destitute, it follows that because a man is destitute he's a drunk. *Non sequitur* has been a popular road to fallacy through the ages. A circle, or so it is argued, is a perfect shape; it follows that because God is perfect and God made the universe the orbit of the earth round the sun must be a circle (in fact, it is an ellipse). *Post hoc* is another form of fallacy when, for example, it is concluded that Lisbon was destroyed by an earthquake in 1755 because of the wickedness of the population. But perhaps the most attractive way of constructing a fallacy is what the logicians call the *fallacy of many questions*, in which the question which you do ask carries within itself an assumption which may or may not be true. A version of this approach is: 'Answer yes or no. Have you stopped beating your wife?'

The verbal route to fallacy, depending on the sloppy use of words, is nearly as wide-ranging as the material route. *Equivocation*, for example, arises when two meanings of the same word are muddled up together. It does *not* follow that because all fair things are honourable, this blonde is honourable because she is fair. *Amphibology* is another splendid road to confusion. 'He only said that' appears at first sight to be a perfectly clear sentence. It could mean, however, either that he only and nobody else said that, or that the only thing he said was that. Then there are the two ways in which verbal fallacy may occur called *composition* and *division* when, by saying 'the angles of a triangle are less than two right angles' the point is left open as to whether each angle separately or the three angles taken together are less than two right angles. Finally, the use of *accent* is a splendid method of spreading verbal fallacy. 'What a fool you are' addressed to an acquaintance can range all the way from rank abuse to an affectionate suggestion that the individual addressed is a delightful and witty person – depending on how the sentence is accented.

Perhaps, if we know what we are doing, a fallacy in its place may be harmless. Nevertheless, it is useful to be aware that students of logic have thought about fallacies and identified so many ways of crooked thinking.

CROWDED LIVING

Those people who fear that dire results will ensue from the growth, particularly during recent years, of the numbers of the human species (see 'Population Explosion') have also convinced themselves that dreadful things will happen to society, as they have been shown to do among animals, from the very fact of crowding. Experiments with rats, mice and other animals as well have shown that when they are kept in a tub or some other confined space, given plenty to eat and drink, and encouraged to breed, as their numbers increase a point is reached when their adrenal glands become enlarged, the activity of the gonads of the males diminishes, the average size of each successive generation becomes smaller and the social behaviour of the colony breaks down.

The remarkable and distressing happenings among experimental animals has been taken to apply to people. Crowd them up too densely, it is said, and they will go the way of the rats and mice. Indeed, some of the troubles we already see – mugging, rape and riots in the streets – are, it is suggested, due to population density.

I now propose to suggest (supported by a scholarly paper published by Peter Newman and Trevor Hogan from Western Australia) that this widely held belief is a fallacy.

To start with, many of the places where street violence and other indications of social disruption are most apparent, are not particularly overcrowded. The average number of people per hectare in New York is only 26, and in the cities of the United States as a whole it is 15. And the United States is a violent place. Historically, the urban density of cities in Europe and Asia, long before rats and mice were brought into the equation, ranged from 100 to 200 people per hectare and some were very much more heavily populated. For example, in 430 BC there were somewhere about 300 citizens per hectare in Babylon, yet no reference to their adrenal glands being enlarged has survived. And in Rome in AD 100 there were 500 people per hectare. In the Middle Ages, the population density in Genoa was somewhere about 600 per hectare, and in 1750 the figures suggest that the density was nearly the same in Edinburgh.

Today many European cities have a population density between 100 and 200 people per hectare. While the density in Hong Kong, where vigour and the effective operation of the men's gonads are unchallenged, is 347 per hectare, compared with Calcutta at 303.

In spite of these contradictory figures, it is the generally accepted view of community leaders, town planners and other members of the intelligentsia that people would do better if they were spaced further apart. Because Lorenz, Wynn-Edwards and a number of other distinguished zoologists have shown that when animals have too little space, an increase in aggression and a breakdown of social order takes place, it has become an item of received doctrine that the same must hold for people. It now appears that this may not only be a fallacy so far as human beings are concerned but that it may not apply universally among animals. Birds and fishes often possess pronounced territoriality (that is, they demand their own space) whereas chimpanzees, orang-utangs and gorillas do not.

Regardless of what the generality of town planners have thought up till now, there is little relationship between such indications of social disorder as the crime rate, delinquency, poor educational performance, suicide and drug-taking and urban overcrowding, when one considers high-density cities such as Tokyo, Singapore and Hong Kong and low-density American and Australian towns. Furthermore, while the population density in American and European cities has been falling over the last few decades, this has not been accompanied by any fall in social disorder; indeed, there is some evidence to the contrary.

Even the notion that, whether or not high-density living gives rise to social breakdown, crowding is unhealthy may also be a fallacy. Perhaps in the fourteenth century one was more likely to die of the Black Death in a crowded city, or to succumb to the plague in seventeenth century London. By 1898, when Ebeneza Howard was preaching the virtues of low-density living in 'garden cities', his argument for their benefits on the grounds not only of social virtues but also of health, was already doubtful. Today, when running water and sewage disposal systems are commonplace and there is scientific understanding of water-borne diseases and much else in the field of hygiene, health in high-density cities is fully as good as that in rural areas and frequently better. This has been dramatically shown in Third World cities which attract people in large numbers even to poverty in the cities from the worse poverty and distress of the country.

The idea that high-density cities are bad and low-density ones, as found in many parts of the United States, in Australia and New Zealand and as 'New Towns' in Great Britain – Milton Keynes and Telford, for example – good, is mainly restricted to the English-speaking world. Those who study these 'improvements' are beginning to notice that the spreading out of people thus can perhaps be blamed for the callousness which one citizen shows for another which is less noticeable in the denser spacing of the population of the older, longer-established cities of Europe. It is now being discovered, even by experts brought up in the belief in spreading people out and that a city should be made as close an imitation of the country as possible (or at least be a 'garden city'), that crowding brings people together which, contrary to modern dogma, is good.

The fallacy of the accepted belief that high-density crowding (if it is indeed that) is bad and the extended low-density, Los Angeles- or Milton Keynes-type city is good can most glaringly be seen when one comes to consider the matter of transport. Venice and Genoa, Paris and Rome are high-density places, to be sure. They were built to be walked about in. The new cities of America, the 'new towns' of Great Britain and the suburbs of almost everywhere cannot be lived in with any satisfaction without the possession of a motor-car. At the present time, although half the families of the new low-density towns and suburbs possess a motor-car, this implies that the other half suffer the social disadvantage of not having one while at the same time having to cope with all those nuisances arising from motor traffic in their city.

How surprising it is that only now are we coming to realize that to consider that city life, with people closely side by side on each hectare, as they are in Genoa, Rome, Bath and Paris, must be socially disruptive, is a fallacy.

CRYOGENICS

As long ago as 1776, the great British physiologist, John Hunter, having just carried out an experiment demonstrating that the idea of freezing an animal and then bringing it back to life was not practical, wrote thus: 'Till this time I had imagined that it might be possible to prolong life to any period by freezing a person . . . as I thought all action and waste would cease until the body was thawed. I thought that if a man would give up the last ten years of his life to this kind of alternate oblivion and action, it might be prolonged to a thousand years; and by getting himself thawed every hundred years he might learn what happened during his frozen condition. Like other schemers, I thought I should make a fortune by it; but this experiment undeceived me.'

The possibility of being able to prolong life and cheat death has always appealed to the popular imagination. The fact that the life of seeds and of micro-organisms can apparently be extended virtually indefinitely in Arctic regions implied that life, even if at a lower level than the life of man, can indeed be extended by freezing. Nevertheless, in spite of the qualified popularity of Life Extension Societies and the apparently serious proposal that astronauts should be frozen to accomplish manned interstellar voyages taking centuries, there is no conclusive evidence to suggest that such a procedure is feasible and that the possibility of freezing people to be thawed and resuscitated later on is anything other than a fallacy. Dr Hunter got it right, it seems, in 1776.

Death has never been popular in the United States. The main purpose of an American funeral is to pretend that the 'dear departed' is still alive. Towards that purpose, the corpse is dressed in his or her best clothes, beauticians in the employ of the morticians exert their considerable skills to give the corpse's face a healthy life-like appearance, the lid of the coffin is left open so that the corpse can take part in the funeral ceremony until the last possible moment, and the coffin itself is made to be as watertight as possible to protect the inmate from decay and corruption for as long as possible. The latest development in this process is cryogenics. That is to say, the dying – if they can afford it – are given the opportunity of being frozen and subsequently maintained in perpetuity in the frozen state. The object of this procedure is to allow them to be brought back to body temperature should advances in medicine have achieved new discoveries providing a cure for the malady from which they died in the first place. There are two fallacies underlying this notion, rendering it virtually certain that those investing the considerable sums involved in having themselves frozen will lose their money.

Scientific research has undoubtedly made progress in finding means whereby certain human cells can be maintained in a viable state over long periods of time. Some success has been achieved with blood cells and greater success in freezing semen. This, however, requires the addition of glycerol or some other solvent to prevent damage due to the formation of ice crystals. Tissue taken from the thyroid and certain other organs has also been maintained frozen and successfully thawed when glycerol is used.

Hibernating animals are not in a frozen state. If the body temperature of a golden hamster falls below freezing the animal dies. And even when the animal's body temperature is maintained above freezing, the hibernating creature may suffer from frostbite if its extremities become too cold.

Kidneys, hearts and other human organs used for transplantation, whether they are contributed by a living donor, as kidneys are, or, like hearts, taken from a dead one, are kept cool but they cannot successfully be frozen. It seems that although certain simpler cells and tissues, such as eye corneas stored in a 'cornea bank', can survive carefully controlled applications of low temperature, more complex combinations of tissues, quite apart from whole human bodies, cannot. If those wealthy Americans who invest money in having their dead bodies frozen, applied equal judgement to this investment as they did to the management of their finances that made them rich, they would be compelled to admit that the whole business was based on a fallacy. The cells in the skin of a man's chin can survive his falling into a crevasse in a glacier. When after years have passed, he turns up in the moraine at the bottom, his beard will have grown. The man himself, however, though fresh and undecayed, will be dead.

The second fallacy in wanting after death to have oneself put into cold storage is to expect that, even if a healthy man frozen could be recovered equally healthy when thawed out some years later – which is a fallacious hope anyway – it is surely doubly fallacious to expect that the disease that led to the death of a sick old man can be treatable then. The main thrust of medical science is to *prevent* heart disease, stroke or cancer; what can it be expected to do with a thawed-out Rip van Winkle with blocked cardiac arteries, damaged cerebral circulation or malign tumours – even assuming that the frozen individual was not killed in a road accident? No. I'm afraid that John Hunter definitely got it right in 1776.

DOWSING

A widespread faith exists in the power which some people claim to possess to detect the presence of underground water where it was not previously known to be. Nevertheless, I am prepared to relegate dowsing to the realms of fallacy. If, later on, I am convincingly proved to be wrong, I shall be happy to delete this article from any later edition of my *Dictionary of Fallacies*.

The art of using a divining rod for the discovery of something hidden dates back to immemorial antiquity. There was, for example, the *virgula divina* used for taking auguries by means of throwing down a bunch of sticks, as described by Cicero and Tacitus, whereby the gods would tell the diviner what he wanted to know through the pattern made by the sticks on the ground. The use of a forked twig of hazel or willow was described by Agricola in a book published in 1540. Before that, in the fifteenth century, miners in the Harz mountains in Germany used a dowsing or divining rod when prospecting for minerals. The idea of thus using a forked twig attracted the attention of merchant adventurers of Queen Elizabeth's time who brought it home for trial by Cornish tin miners. Only when mining declined in Cornwall was its use transferred to the search for underground water.

Just as those attempting to divine the future might use either the pattern formed by a bundle of sticks thrown onto the ground or the shape assumed by a sheep's intestines thrown over the left shoulder, so also do those who still believe in dowsing use indifferently a forked hazel or willow twig, a fork cut from a holly bush, a piece of wire or even a forked wand made from copper tubing. As they prowl about the area which they are searching, the dowsers feel a twitch and the twig twists in their hands where, if they have got it right, water is to be found – if the well-diggers dig deep enough.

Faith in the efficacy of this performance persists and, even in our present technological age, professional dowsers are in business whose clients are happy to pay their fees. There are, however, sceptics – of whom I am one – who argue that evidence is seldom sought as to whether water might not also be found should other drillings be made, if not at random, at least in places where it could reasonably be expected to be located without the need for any dowsing ritual. Further, the sceptics say that to promulgate the hypothesis that the twitching of the rod is due to 'motor automation' excited by a 'reflex action' triggered by some mysterious 'stimulus' emanating from the underground water, is to wrap up the ceremony of dowsing in a series of ambiguities for the existence of which there is no evidence.

In contrast to the mysteries of dowsing are the modern advances of geology, a part of which is hydrography, the science dealing with all the waters of the earth's surface, together with hydrology and hydrogeology concerned with water on and in the earth's crust. From such scientific studies comes the delineation of aquifers, underground stores of water within the geological structures underlying the landscape. Pursuing researches into hydrogeology, French scientists were able to drill deep wells and find water in the Sahel, the arid lands lying south of the Sahara desert. In England, other researchers have recently mapped the sources of the hot springs in the city of Bath within the area between Bath and Bristol. This, surely, is the use of reason to understand the problems of earth and the waters under the earth without reference to the vestiges of earlier times when divining rods and animal intestines were used to unravel the omens and auguries of a dark, cruel world.

Even though one study (and there are more) does not necessarily establish proof, I am prepared to attach weight to the report of an experience with a dowser near Sydney in Australia in 1982. Malcolm McDowell, the owner of a farm, was anxious to obtain water for his livestock. He arranged to obtain, firstly, the services of an experienced professional water diviner, Vic Vaisey, and, at the same time, the advice of the New South Wales Water Resources Commission. The diviner came to the farm, spent an hour walking backwards and forwards with his divining rod and divined the presence of two underground streams, one running east and west at a depth of 35 feet and another running north and south at a depth of 40 feet. He marked the spot on the surface under which he claimed that the two streams crossed.

The Water Resources Commission, after studying a map of the farm, sent Mr McDowell a report suggesting that water might be present in the strata under the surface at a depth of between 50 and 330 feet with the most promising depth at 200 feet.

When drilling was carried out at the spot indicated by Vic Vaisey, no water was found at 35 or 40 feet and dry shale continued to a depth of over 80 feet. When, however, drilling was continued further to a depth of 210 feet, a flow of 130 gallons of water an hour was struck, which increased to 250 gallons an hour when the bore reached a depth of 220 feet.

In an earlier controlled trial in Rome, reported in 1979, four dowsers were unable to locate buried pipes through which running water was passing, in spite of an offer of a prize of ten thousand dollars to any of them who could succeed in doing so.

DREAMS

There are two kinds of fallacies about dreams. Firstly there are those arising from the distant past which assume that dreams are much more important than they really are. The second group of fallacies are held by those who consider that dreams are of little or no importance at all.

(1) *Oneiromancy* From the days of remote antiquity people have been puzzled by the nature of dreams and have constructed theories about their significance. Throughout history there have been soothsayers who have pretended to possess the ability to interpret dreams. Many of these interpretations have claimed to be of prophetic significance and to forecast what the future holds for the dreamer. Although a skilful practitioner of the art of oneiromancy, as it is called, can make some sort of reasonable prediction about what is likely to happen in the future, just as the rest of us can, it is clearly a fallacy to believe that a dream possesses any magical predictive significance – regardless of the persuasive plausibility of Joseph's interpretation of Pharaoh's dreams, as described in the Book of

Exodus. It will be recalled that the fatness or leanness of cattle in the monarch's dreams was claimed to be an indication of the weather in Egypt during the subsequent fourteen years. Regardless of the obvious uselessness of dreams as a means of meteorological forecasting, as in other areas of prophecy, there are still unsophisticated people today who take exponents of oneiromancy seriously and buy their 'dream books', by which they hope to interpret such dreams as they may have.

(2) *Dreams and well-being* In spite of the fact that some credulous people have stuck to an indefensible belief in oneiromancy, most sensible individuals no longer have faith in the predictive properties of dreams. Next came Sigmund Freud, whose book, *The Interpretation of Dreams*, was published in Germany in 1900. Freud's basic idea was that dreams should be understood as an expression of the longings, desires, wishes and urges of the dreamer. Often these are balked wishes and frustrated yearnings which the dreamer would not allow himself to harbour if he were awake. For half a century, Freud's teachings were debated by psychologists, some of whom believed in their validity and some of whom did not. By the 1950s, interest in his ideas had waned and, except for a few specialists, most people had come to the opinion that dreams, although they might be an interesting area of study, were of little importance. Amongst these sceptics there were those prepared to assert that they never dreamt at all. But such beliefs – that dreams are unimportant and that there are people who never dream – are fallacies too.

It is odd to have to recall that, in spite of all the interest taken in dreams over the ages, perhaps the most important observation about them was not made until 1950. It was then noticed that there are two kinds of sleep. These are most readily observed with the aid of an electroencephalograph (EEG), an instrument for recording the electrical rhythms of the brain. The recordings during wakefulness change gradually as the person under examination goes to sleep. The kind of tracings recorded during this time are called those of 'orthodox sleep'. After about ninety minutes of orthodox sleep, the EEG readings change to something like those obtained during wakefulness although the person being studied is fast asleep. At the same time the sleeper's eyes start moving about behind his closed eyelids. These EEG recordings are said to be those of 'paradoxical sleep', or of those characteristic of rapid eye movement (REM). During a typical night's sleep, a sleeper will oscillate from orthodox sleep to REM sleep four or five times. In general, orthodox sleep occupies about 80 per cent of the 7 hours 20 minutes of an average night's sleep. The remaining 20 per cent, occupying 88 minutes, which is quite a long time, is spent in REM sleep.

The interesting point is this. If people are woken up during the periods of orthodox sleep, they will always be found not to have been dreaming. On the other hand, when they are roused from REM sleep, they are always in the middle of a dream, even those who, if left to have their sleep out, will claim not to have been dreaming at all. It thus appears that everyone dreams for quite long periods, whether he or she remembers dreaming or not. According to a comprehensive French survey, ordinary men and women between the ages of thirty and eighty sleep on average for the 7 hours 20 minutes which I have already mentioned. It is a mistake to imagine that, once childhood is passed, older people sleep any less than younger ones. Nor does exercise or IQ make much difference, unless the IQ is very low, when people tend to sleep longer. Most striking of all is the fact that, whether people remember their dreams or not, all of us dream for about an hour and a half each night.

In spite of all the research that has been done on sleep, its function is still unknown. What *is* known, however, is that sleep is essential. The maximum time that anyone can remain without sleep is approximately eight days and eight hours, that is, 200 hours. By the third day of wakefulness, derangement of behaviour, including unreasonable laughter and quarrelsomeness, occurs. After the third day, mental derangement becomes more exaggerated. Wild suspicions occur; the victims believe that those around them are plotting against them, that their food is poisoned, that the floor is heaving. Such hallucinations persist until the urge to sleep becomes overpowering.

These are the effects of depriving a man or woman of sleep entirely. In 1960, however, an experiment was done to study the effect of allowing people to sleep but not to dream. As soon as

REM sleep occurred, the sleepers were woken up. When they were allowed to go to sleep again, their sleep was at first orthodox. During the first night, it was found necessary to wake them up four or five times. By the fifth night, however, twenty or thirty periods of REM sleep occurred at the onset of which they had to be woken. Most remarkable of all, however, was the fact that, although these people enjoyed seven hours of orthodox sleep a night, they developed all the symptoms of people deprived of sleep altogether. The conclusion can thus be drawn that mankind has to dream. Dreams may have no significance in foreseeing the future, as common sense would imply, but they are not only important in everyday life, they are universal and essential.

DRINKS LIKE A FISH

The picturesque description of an intemperate individual who is constantly imbibing alcoholic beverages as being one who 'drinks like a fish' is a fallacy. A fish drinks no more in proportion to its size than any other animal. The notion that it does is based on the mistaken idea that a goldfish in a bowl, let us say, or a carp in a pond, continuously pursing its lips and oscillating its throat, is drinking. What it is actually doing is pumping a stream of water through its gills. There is oxygen dissolved in this water, and the fish needs oxygen to live, just as we do. We constantly breathe and, in the aquatic environment in which it lives, the fish constantly pumps water through its gills.

Not every living thing needs oxygen. Yeast, for example, can live without it, but when it does it only uses its food, malt sugars, let us say, very inefficiently and leaves what some people might consider the best part, namely alcohol, behind. It was a big step forward in evolution when, firstly, green plants evolved capable of using light to release oxygen into the air and, secondly, animals developed the ability to use it. The most effective animals, including ourselves, took to living on dry land, where the oxygen was easiest to get at. Many others remained living in water, but developed gills enabling them to make use of oxygen dissolved in the water. But they are not drinking when they do this, they are breathing.

EARRINGS

The fallacies relating to earrings fall into the category of beliefs for which there is no evidence but which those who have faith in them *wish* were true. Wishing something to be true does not make it so. It is therefore pitiful to find that even today, when we enjoy so many benefits from science, which is strictly rational and firmly based on observation and measurement, there are still people prepared to believe the irrational.

The most widely held fallacy about earrings is that by wearing them suspended from holes pierced through the lobes of the ears, eyesight will be improved. Yet there is no rational reason to suggest that by making such a minor mutilation to the fleshy dependency of the outer ear the optic nerve can in any way be affected. Reason, however, has little to do with belief in the optical efficacy of earrings. Those who support the fallacy base their faith on magical rather than rational grounds. For example, the *Exeter and Plymouth Gazette* of 13 March 1877 reports that if earrings are to improve the wearer's eyesight, they must have been gifts from a man (not a woman) and must be accepted without the donor being thanked.

Adherence to the fallacy relating earrings to eyesight is strongest among sailors. In some places, it is also believed that the wearing of earrings is a protection against being drowned. Here we see in its strongest form the hope that something totally irrational could be true is true. Sailors are better aware than other men of the danger and unpredictability of life. Even in our own times, when science has provided navigators with radar and ship-to-shore communication, ships founder each year and sailors are drowned. Although it is deplorable that credence should be given to fallacy, it is understandable that there should be those who, finding certain help nowhere else, find comfort in what tougher minds can clearly see to be untruth. It is interesting to recall that Nelson, a seaman of unequalled professionalism, ruled that his sailors should dispense with their earrings, regardless of any faith in their protective power, on the strictly rational grounds that by giving their opponents something to take hold of, they were a handicap in hand-to-hand fighting.

It is possible that the basis of this ridiculous fallacy, i.e. that by piercing one's ears and putting earrings through them one's eyesight could be improved, arose from a *non sequitur*, that is, a wrong conclusion being placed on a valid observation.

There is in ophthalmology a condition called 'second sight'. What happens is that as people grow older, just as the shape of their jaws change and their dentures need renewing, so also may the shape of the lenses within their eyes change. It can follow that, after having been short-sighted for years, they come to see better. If they attribute this improvement in vision to their earrings, their belief in the fallacy linking them to eye-sight will be reinforced.

ELEPHANTS NEVER FORGET

The general belief that an elephant has a good memory is, perhaps, not a matter of much significance. Yet for those who consider it best to support beliefs which are founded on proper evidence rather than be prepared unthinkingly to accept popular assumptions, it is worth examining what evidence – if any – may be available to support even such a trivial idea as that relating to the elephant.

An elephant is a big animal and, as might be expected, has a bigger brain than many smaller creatures. It possesses, in fact, approximately 1lb of brain for each 100lbs of body weight. But then a gorilla has about 1lb of brain for each 140lbs of body weight, and a man 1lb of brain to about 70lbs of body weight. There is, therefore, little in this evidence to support the hypothesis that elephants are conspicuously intellectual or that their memories are especially retentive.

Circus elephants are capable of learning a variety of tricks and remembering what they have learnt. Again, however, the tricks they do are not particularly sophisticated. Working elephants in Burma can be trained to pull and push and pick up logs. This, however, differs little from the sort of work which oxen can be taught to do, and no one comments on their powers of mental recall. Elephants become attached to their handlers and remember them, but so do dogs, about whose memories no special claims are made. Dr Raymond Ditmars reported the case of an elephant in the New York Zoological Park which persisted in a violent dislike of one of the keepers, but there are dogs which behave similarly.

None of this evidence justifies the assumption, as a proved fact worthy of note by an educated community, that, compared with other animals, elephants possess particularly good memories.

FAKES

The fallacies by which people can become entrapped are of various kinds. In ancient times, there was an excuse for those beset by the problems of a dangerous and uncertain life believing in what seemed to be the ordered procession of the planets as interpreted by astrology, although today we can see that astrology is nonsense, as described earlier. There was less excuse for the guardians of the temple pretending that their carefully engineered miracles, organized to strengthen the faith of believers, were true manifestations of the gods; while today we rightly impugn as charlatans those who contrive artificial UFOs. The belief in many fallacies derives from simple error and a misreading or ignorance of the truth. Fallacy can, however, also arise from human deceit. Sensible people must always bear in mind that there are those who contrive fakes with the express purpose to deceive. Against these we citizens, whether we are scientists or not, must be on our guard.

(1) *Piltdown Man* In 1913 a report appeared in the *Quarterly Journal* of the Geological Society of London describing the discovery, by a Mr Charles Dawson, an amateur geologist, of the fragments of a skull and a lower jaw and teeth in a gravel pit near the village of Piltdown in Sussex. These pieces of bone had been found, it was stated, in 1908 but it was not until four years later, when Arthur Woodward, an expert from the British Museum, had judged them to be up to 65 million years old that the scientific world was made aware of their existence. The importance of these discoveries and others brought to light afterwards from the Piltdown gravel, was that they seemed to provide evidence of a 'missing link', a creature midway between man and ape.

For forty years, Piltdown Man was accepted as evidence for an unexpected line of evolution along which the human species had developed. Then, in 1949, Dr Kenneth Oakley initiated a study of the Piltdown fragments. His initial results were inconclusive. By 1953, however, he was able to show that whereas the pieces of skull were a few thousand years old – but nothing like 65 million years – and were from a human head, the jawbone was that of a modern orang-utang. In short, the whole thing was a fake. Clearly, it had been carefully prepared by someone with a great deal of knowledge and skill. The purpose of this elaborate fake and, indeed, the name of the perpetrator have never been clearly established.

(2) *The Vinland Map* In 1957 Laurence Witton, an American dealer in antiquarian books, announced that during a visit to Europe he had acquired a manuscript entitled *The Tartar Relation*. Bound up with this was a fifteenth-century map, *Vinlanda Insula*, of parts of North America of which there had previously been no known information. On this map was the inscription, 'discovered by Bjarni and Leif in company'. Here then was documentary evidence of the discovery of mainland America by Europeans before Christopher Columbus.

Witton showed this map to Alexander Victor, curator of maps at Yale University, and to Thomas Marston, a recognized expert in medieval manuscripts. After eight years study, the Yale University Press published their results. In this scholarly work, Victor concluded that a scribe had copied the map from an earlier record made in 1440 and that it 'contains the earliest known and indisputable cartographic representation of any part of the Americas'. Experts from the British Museum supported these conclusions.

The fact that Witton would never divulge the source from which he had obtained the manuscript with the Vinland Map in it, continued to disturb certain scholars. It was, therefore, not surprising that in 1975, when new methods for assessing the age of manuscripts had become available, it was submitted to renewed examination. The manuscript did, it appeared, date from the fifteenth century. As for the map, however, the ink with which it was drawn was seen to have been prepared no earlier than 1920. The Vinland Map, with which the world of scholarship had been deceived for eighteen years, was a fake.

(3) *Richard of Cirencester's Roman Britain* Charles Bertram, currently described in the *Encyclopaedia Britannica* as an 'English literary imposter', published in 1757 a forgery purporting to be a map drawn by a certain Richard of Cirencester, a minor fourteenth-century scholar. Bertram, who was 24 at the time, showed his map

to William Stukeley, a distinguished antiquary of the times, who accepted it as genuine. Next, the Royal Ordnance Survey copied the bogus sites of Roman stations on to their maps where they remained for a hundred and nine years. It was not until 1866 that the imposture was exposed. It was observed that the text of *De Situ Britanniae*, the document of which Bertram's map was a part, contained quotations from Tacitus taken from an edition not published until two centuries after Richard of Cirencester's death. The manuscript itself was made up of chunks taken from Caesar, Selinus, Tacitus and other writers. And so the Ordnance Survey maps had to be changed again. A palpable fake produced in 1757 had been accepted virtually unchallenged until 1866.

(4) *The Vermeers of Hans van Meegeren* The case of Hans van Meegeren is in some respects one of the most remarkable examples of faking ever to be recorded. Here we have a painter whose own work was ignored and who suffered from his lack of success and public acclaim, but whose paintings in the style of Vermeer were so excellent that they were universally accepted by collectors and experts alike as having been painted by Vermeer. This allowed van Meegeren, firstly, twisted satisfaction at the expense of the connoisseurs who had failed to recognize his own talents; secondly, money from the sale of his forgeries; and, thirdly, patriotic satisfaction at being able to fob off his reproductions to German generals. The final twist to the story was his defence against the charge of selling his country's treasures to the enemy by painting another 'Vermeer' in all the publicity of his prison cell.

After the end of World War II, the Dutch authorities set out to retrieve the artistic masterpieces which had been looted from their galleries during the enemy occupation. In the course of this search, they ran across a splendid painting by Jan Vermeer entitled 'Christ and the Adulteress' which had been in the possession of Hermann Goering. The authorities were, however, at a loss to know where it had come from. In due course, they traced it to the middle-aged dealer, Hans van Meegeren. He claimed that he had acquired the painting from an impoverished Italian family who wished to remain anonymous. In due course, however, van Meegeren found himself charged with collaborating with the enemy and selling national works of art. Faced with the possibility of penal servitude for life, he signed a confession that it was he who had painted not only 'Christ and the Adulteress' but thirteen other classical Dutch masterpieces by 'Vermeer' and 'Peter de Hooch'. The art world was astounded and refused to believe him, particularly since he claimed to have painted 'The Disciples of Emmaus' which had caused a sensation when it was bought by the Boymans Museum in Rotterdam for 500,000 guilders and exhibited as the central attraction in an exhibition marking Queen Wilhelmina's jubilee. This 'early work by Vermeer' had been hailed as 'a miracle of painting' by many of the critics. Besides the skill he had devoted to the painting, van Meegeren had taken equal trouble to use, wherever possible, the same pigments and varnish as those employed by Vermeer; he had developed a technique for ageing his paintings by heating them in a kiln; and he had inserted small flaws and signs of damage, which the gallery subsequently 'restored' before putting the pictures on display.

To prove his innocence, van Meegeren sat in his prison cell and painted another masterpiece, 'Jesus in the Temple', in the style of Vermeer. He was acquitted of trading with the enemy but found guilty of fraud and sentenced to one year's imprisonment. But before he could serve his sentence, he died, a sad monument to trickery and a warning to all of us of the subtlety of excellence and the fragility of truth.

FOOD AND NUTRITION

1. *Brain food* The idea that eating fish is good for the brain is a fallacy. Eskimos, Icelanders and Norwegians, all of whom eat a diet containing a substantial proportion of fish, are no cleverer than anybody else. This fallacy does possess a respectable – if mistaken – scientific background. During the nineteenth century, chemists turned their attention seriously to the analysis of different organs of the body, on the one hand, and to the chemical composition of the various foods of which the diet is composed, on the other. It was

observed that the human brain is particularly rich in the element phosphorus. It was also noticed that fish, and particularly fish such as sardines, anchovies and canned salmon, of which it is customary to eat the bones, contained more phosphorus than many other articles of diet. These two facts were put together to arrive at the mistaken conclusion that fish was therefore specifically a brain food.

There are two good reasons why this is not so. The first is that the body does not work as simply as this. If the food you eat supplies as much phosphorus as you need, which, provided one's diet is a normal one, it is virtually sure to do, extra phosphorus will not produce any effect. Secondly, one's bones are the main reservoir of phosphorus in the body. It would, therefore, be as sensible, rather than claiming fish to be good for the brain, to argue that it is better for the skeleton. Another oddity about the fallacy of fish being a brain food is why fish? Cheese, for example, is richer in phosphorus. Yet nobody, so far as I am aware, has ever claimed that eating Cheddar or Stilton influences one's intellectual performance.

2. *Eggs* There are at least two widely current fallacies about eggs. The first is that brown eggs are more nourishing than white ones. The second is that the eggs from hens allowed to range freely about the barnyard are better in some way than those from hens raised in batteries.

The colour of an egg's shell has no bearing on the nutritional value of the egg itself. It is entirely a matter of race. There are some breeds of hens that lay brown-shelled eggs and there are some that lay white-shelled eggs. Civilized people today do not judge men and women on the basis of skin colour, neither is there any reason for them to judge hens on the colour of the shells of their eggs – particularly as the shell is the one part which nobody ever eats.

If the hen does not get *enough* to eat, it will probably go off lay altogether. When it does lay, the composition of its food has only a minor influence on the nutritional value of its eggs. The feed may affect to some degree the *colour* of the yolk. Free-range birds, if they have the opportunity, will pick up greenstuff which can influence the colour of the yolks of their eggs and give them a stronger yellow tint. This yellow pigment contributes to the vitamin A activity of the eggs. On the other hand, the composition of the feed provided for intensively reared birds is so prepared, by the addition of dried grass and other ingredients, as to ensure its adequate nutrient content. A possible problem with eggs from free-ranging hens is that they may become dirty in rainy weather. Should the eggs have to be washed, their shells become less resistant to infection by contaminating micro-organisms.

There are people who, after having finished eating a soft-boiled egg and scraped out the last morsel, jab their egg-spoon through the bottom of the shell. They may not know it, but when they do this they are keeping up a fallacy derived from ancient times. In the distant past, it was believed that if a man's enemies gained possession of the leavings of his food, the main part of which, through being eaten, had become his very flesh, they could cast a spell over them and thus do him harm. By breaking a hole through the shell, the efficacy of any such spell could be foiled.

3. *Energy* It is not altogether surprising that many people have fallacious ideas about foods which, they believe, give them 'energy'. The scientists themselves are principally to blame for this fallacy. It is they who, by measuring the fuel value of foods, first in calories and, in recent times, in kilojoules, gave ordinary people the wrong idea. To be sure, both these units are measures of energy well understood by engineers. But they are less well understood by the general public. To an engineer, 'energy' means 'the power of doing work'. This is different from what ordinary people understand it to mean or, indeed, what it meant back in the eighteenth century, which was 'vigour of action'. And what 'vigour' meant then, which is what it means now, was 'liveliness'. It is undoubtedly true that chocolate bars, sweet iced cake, butter, jam and mutton fat are all high in energy value. But to believe that such foods 'give you energy' is a fallacy if what is really meant by 'energy' is 'vigour'. A fat man is, by virtue of his obesity, rich in energy-value (just as a car may be full of petrol). He may nevertheless be lacking in vigour (and the car may be sluggish too).

4. *Fast food* It is a general belief, particularly among the intelligentsia, that so-called 'fast food' is junk. This is a fallacy which is

mainly based on snobbery. Even though it is fashionable to pretend that there are nowadays no class distinctions, it has to be admitted that there is less elegance and gentility in carrying away a bagful of hamburgers or a packet of crisps than in being served by a waiter in an expensive restaurant or in sitting down to a formal dinner party. The fallacy has therefore grown up that, because it is popular, cheap and quick, a mass-produced hamburger must be bad for the uncouth crowd who like it, buy it and eat it. The fallacy is self-evident to anyone who stops a moment to think. There are two main components in a hamburger. The first is meat and the second bread, both of which have been esteemed as important and nourishing articles of diet virtually since man began. When to these are added tomato and lettuce, the mixture of ingredients approximates to an almost nutritionally perfect meal for a hungry young man and his girlfriend.

In my youth, fish and chips, which in those days were commonly dispensed in newspaper, were similarly condemned as 'rubbish' by the middle classes. Today, now that fish has become expensive, people have come to accept that this early example of 'fast food' is nourishing as well as tasty.

It is also a fallacy to deprecate crisps as an unhealthy 'fast food' snack. Crisps represent a comparatively concentrated source of nourishment for a hungry boy or girl, yet their bulk tends to prevent their becoming by themselves a complete meal. As such, the fat in which the sliced potato is fried could be undesirably much. Yet the potato contributes protein to the whole and vitamin C as well. Discourage young people from eating crisps, which they like, on the fallacious grounds that they are nutritionally undesirable and you will encourage them to suck sweets which, in excess, are.

5. *Health foods* It is a fallacy to categorize one group of foods, sold by one peculiar class of shop as 'health foods'. This implies that foods not bought from these shops are 'unhealthy foods'. There is every reason why people who have a liking for brown bread, black treacle and apple juice should be able to buy them. Nor should one object to their being able to buy vitamin tablets if they want to. Where there is cause for objection to those who purport to market 'health foods' is when they propagate such fallacies as that, if one

does *not* eat royal jelly, pure lecithin granules and the like, one's 'brain, lungs, nerves, liver, kidneys, bone marrow, glands and heart' will be unable to function efficiently. It is equally a fallacy to claim that if one *does* eat, as a supplement to a normal diet, extra amounts of vitamins and minerals, amino acids, molasses and concentrated roots from the Orient, one may expect to enjoy a superior form of well-being and, in fact, to be healthier than healthy.

6. *Honey* Honey is a very agreeable dietary adjunct, but no more. The queen, as the old rhyme has it, was in the parlour, eating bread and honey. When, in medieval times, sugar was an expensive rarity, honey was virtually the only sweetening agent available to ordinary people. It is, however, a fallacy that it is anything more – which, even though it is a widely held belief, is no less a fallacy.

Golden syrup, to which few people other than hungry schoolboys possessed of a sweet tooth attribute any particular nutritional value, is composed of 77 per cent carbohydrate and 23 per cent water. As these figures show, there is precious little room left for golden syrup or honey to contain very much else. There is 0.3 per cent of protein in golden syrup and 0.4 per cent in honey. White bread contains 7.8 per cent of protein, more than 19 times as much as honey where it is not worth mentioning. But people mistakenly do mention it. Golden syrup contains in small amounts a string of trace minerals. Yet these small amounts are mostly many times the amounts present in honey. Search has been made in honey for thirteen different vitamins and tiny traces of two of these have been determined. There are, in fact, 0.05mg of riboflavin and 0.20mg of nicotinic acid in 100g. Yet in corned beef, a nourishing food but one seldom claimed to possess magical health-giving properties, there are 0.23mg of riboflavin and 2.50mg of nicotinic acid per 100g.

7. *Hay diet* Every now and then, a new diet is launched on the public which is claimed to contribute some peculiar benefit or combat some real or – as often happens – some imaginary ill. One of these diets which, in its time in the 1930s, enjoyed a certain misguided popularity, was the Hay diet, promulgated by a Mr W. H. Hay. This is an example of fallacy of which it is all too certain that we have not seen the last; there will be other fallacious diets to come

just as unfounded. Somehow or other, Mr Hay, having learnt that the digestive agent in one's saliva, ptyalin, operates under alkaline conditions, while the digestive enzymes in one's stomach are active under acid conditions, came to the conclusion that acid was bad, regardless of the fact that digestion in the stomach must always function under quite strongly acid conditions. His fallacy was perhaps most perversely stated thus: 'Life, vitality, health, are synonyms for alkalinity . . . When the causes of disease are understood to be simply an accumulation of the acid end-products of digestion . . . then will the huge mortality . . . sink to almost vanishing point.'

Good judgement and the avoidance of fallacy require the sensible man to inform himself of the basic facts of any matter, whether it be economics, astronomy – or diet.

8. *Love* It is common for a young man, anxious to stimulate the love of a young woman, to take her out to dinner. Yet he does not necessarily attribute any particular potency as a stimulant to love to the individual foods of which the chosen menu is composed. Once upon a time, however, in the sixteenth and seventeenth centuries, not long after it had been introduced into Europe from America, the tomato was known as the 'love apple' and was thought to stimulate love-making. At other times, a variety of other foods have been claimed to possess similar potency. One of these was oysters, another was leeks, because their shape was taken to have some phallic significance. The mandrake, which is a plant native to the Mediterranean, features in the Bible as food for love in a passage in the Book of Genesis in which Rachel and Leah squabble over the mandrakes collected by Reuben. Shakespeare also has Cleopatra in one play and Othello in another discussing their alleged activity. The start of the idea was due to the fact that the mandrake root often divides into two parts and thus resembles a man's crotch. Unfortunately, the notion that these and many others are foods for love is a fallacy.

9. *Meat* It is generally believed by men, with the support of their self-sacrificing wives, that meat is a food that gives them strength. Unluckily for the men, who usually like meat and are quite pre-

pared to accept the sacrifices of those who give up the lion's share of the family meat supply for the breadwinner, the notion that eating meat is particularly conducive to the development of muscle-power is a fallacy. Clearly, if a man is to do heavy physical work, he does it best if he is properly fed. This, however, does not mean that he *needs* meat. There are plenty of healthy, muscular vegetarians. Meat is an attractive and, in its proper place, a nourishing food. There is, however, no scientific evidence relating it either to the performance of muscular work or to masculinity. To believe otherwise is a fallacy.

10. *Mother's cake-making* Many a middle-aged person, looking back to the ever-receding days of youth, can be heard to say with a nostalgic sigh, 'Nobody nowadays can bake a cake the way my mother could'. This statement is very often fallacious. There are two reasons why this should be so. The first is that our earliest memories, particularly of pleasant events, remain most vivid in our minds over the years. Could mother's cake, as it was all that long time ago, be presented to us now, it might seem stodgy and un-interesting. Secondly, as time passes, the receptors by which we record taste and smell become fewer and less sensitive. It follows that cake, as judged by our middle-aged senses, *does* taste less interesting than did the cakes of our youth. It does not follow, how-ever, that it *is* less good.

11. *Potatoes* Almost from the time that it was first brought from South America to Europe in the sixteenth century, the potato has been a focus for injurious fallacy. First of all, because the potato, unlike any other crop then known, was a white tuber with bulbous finger-like growths, it recalled the deformed hands and bleached skin of leprosy and was blamed for causing the disease. Later it was accused by a Swiss physician in 1768 of causing scrofula. Next, the fallacy was floated that eating potatoes led to consumption, rickets and fever. These accusations arose from the fact that, as a cheap food, potatoes were eaten by the poorest people among whom such diseases were rife. Finally, potatoes were blamed for causing too many babies to be conceived. This came about because in Ireland, where they were early adopted as the principal food of the people,

large families were the rule. Now, in our own time, potatoes have been blamed for making people fat. One way or another, obesity ensues when people consistently eat more food than they need. It is true that obese people attempting to eat less than they would like to eat, can succeed in part by refusing to eat the roll and, particularly, the butter put so seductively beside their plates by the waiter. They can also usefully refuse potatoes when they are offered. This does not imply that potatoes cause fatness any more than a variety of other foods do. There are many foods far richer than potatoes.

12. *Pills* (as food for the future) It is a common belief of those who watch the advance of science with open-mouthed wonder that some day in the future someone will invent a pill capable of supplying all one needs for the day in the way of nourishment. This is a fallacy. Vitamins and minerals *can* be compressed into a pill, if anyone wants to do such a thing, but when it comes to food itself, the best that can be done, as explorers and the military have already discovered, is to make a dry block weighing something more than ½lb. This comes about because the most concentrated source of energy is fat, providing 9 calories per gram. Since the average person needs about 2500 calories a day, the minimum weight of food, made up from fat, would be 278 grams, which is just over ¼lb. But fat by itself, while supplying the energy to keep the system going, would be uneatable and unbalanced. If, like a slab of pemmican, a food concentrate contained about 20 per cent of protein as well as fat, its energy value would come down to 8 calories per gram. To get 2500 calories from such a mixture, one would have to eat 312 grams. That is about 11oz. Even then, although such an emergency pack might be suitable for an emergency, no one, either now or in the future, would *want* to live on it for any prolonged time. As for a pill – no! It really is a fallacy.

13. *The Protein Gap* The idea of a worldwide 'protein gap' is a peculiar example of a fallacy first put into circulation by the scientific community itself. It was started in 1968 by no less a body than the UN Advisory Committee on the Application of Science and Technology to Development in a report entitled *International Action to Avert the Impending Protein Crisis.* This led to a mighty

effort by a variety of scientific workers to produce high-protein foods for the world's poor. Some of these were prepared with great labour from unconventional sources. There was 'fish flour', protein from petroleum and natural gas, 'texturized vegetable protein' (so-called 'knitted steak') from soya beans, and leaf protein. In the end, after seven years of unquestioning acceptance of what was taken to be a worldwide protein gap, and the expenditure of a great deal of money, after the formation of a UN Protein Advisory Group and the publication by this body of a learned journal, it became clear that the whole notion of a protein gap was a fallacy. In 1975, a comprehensive scientific report was published summarizing the evidence to show that there had never been a world shortage of protein. Here and there – and over too large an area of the globe – what there had been was a shortage of food. The authors of this paper prefaced their report by a quotation attributed to Winston Churchill that 'it is a most nourishing and stimulating diet to eat one's own words'. Perhaps it is most nourishing for scientists.

14. *Vitamins* It was, in some ways, unfortunate that Casimir Funk, back in 1913, decided to call the newly discovered minor components in certain foods, the *absence* of which caused disease, vitamins. There is a magical flavour in the word. Funk can, perhaps, be forgiven when it is recalled that in his day medical science had come to understand that many diseases were due to the *presence* of harmful germs. Today, we are aware that there is, indeed, a group of compounds, some still called Vitamin A, Vitamin B$_1$, Vitamin C and so on, others designated by their chemical names, such as riboflavin, nicotinic acid, pyridoxin and the like, present in different foods in various concentrations, which are required for an adequate diet. This is hard fact; fallacies arise when people step outside fact into make-believe. Two types of fallacy have thus grown up about vitamins. The first has been to attribute to them powers they do not possess. Vitamin E, for example, is recommended as a nostrum for all sorts of ills, some genuine, some imaginary. The facts of the matter are that although the effect of too little Vitamin E can be demonstrated on female rats, little evidence is available to show that people, as distinct from rats, ever show any symptoms of Vitamin E deficiency. Either they do not need dietary Vitamin E at

all or, no matter how peculiar their diet may be, they get enough anyway. Vitamin C has also been claimed to produce beneficial effects when consumed in what are relatively enormous quantities. In particular, it has been reported to prevent those who eat it thus from catching cold. Even though this claim has been supported at length, hard evidence suggests that it is a fallacy.

The second category of fallacy circulated about vitamins is that, even though you may be perfectly healthy eating a fully nutritious diet, should you, on top of this, purchase and consume supplementary supplies of vitamins, you will become healthier still. But I am afraid that this does not happen.

FUNNY BONE

It is a fallacy to describe a particular part of the elbow as the 'funny bone'. It is not a bone at all. Running along the ulna, one of the bones which extends from the elbow to the wrist, is the ulnar nerve. At the elbow, the nerve is situated in a shallow groove not far under the skin. If the elbow is bumped at a particular point, this nerve may be compressed against the bone producing the unmistakable sensation, sending shivers along the arm, of having 'bumped one's funny bone'.

GAMBLER'S LUCK

Gambling can be divided into two categories. People who play serious bridge for money could be said to be gambling, and in a single game there could be a sufficient element of chance in the fall of the cards to allow a novice to defeat a skilful and practised player. But over a sufficient period of time a champion bridge player will always win money from an incompetent opponent. Similarly, among those who bet on horse races there are the punters who take racing seriously and who, by carefully studying form and collecting information about the weather, the health of the horses entered for a particular race, the skill and temperament of the jockeys and all the other relevant factors, can, over a season, compute the performance of individual animals and expect to make money from their bets.

On the other hand, there are games of pure chance, of which roulette is perhaps the best known. Gamblers who indulge in such games can exert no influence on events, yet it is common for them to accept a number of fallacies which, they try to persuade themselves, can influence their success. Players who shoot craps may blow on the dice or speak to them before they make their throw. There is a belief that 'borrowed money cannot lose'; ostensibly sensible people playing roulette may get up, walk three times round their chairs and sit down again in order to 'change their luck'. Perhaps the silliest fallacy among gamblers is their belief that numbers which have come up before influence those which follow. It is common to see roulette players recording in notebooks the result of each spin of the wheel on the assumption that should red come up six times in a row, for example, the next throw is bound to be black. This fallacy arises from a misunderstanding of the mathematical rules of probability. Although the chance of red coming up seven times consecutively is very remote, the chance of red appearing each separate time the wheel is spun is always the same. The odds of heads appearing when tossing a coin is always

50:50 and, even if by some quirk of chance a gambler gets 19 heads in a row, at the twentieth toss the chance of heads appearing is still 50:50.

Where the game is pure chance, the most damaging fallacy a gambler can embrace is the idea that he has discovered a system of winning. The design of a roulette wheel – assuming it to be honest – is such that, in the long run, the certain result is that the casino will win.

GHOSTS

A ghost is, almost by definition, a fallacy. It is an apparition and thus denotes a perception of something which cannot be shown to be occasioned by a real natural object or event. An apparition is usually perceived through the sense of sight, but not always. It may involve the sense of hearing, such as by hollow groans, even – as in Shakespeare's plays – by conversation or, perhaps, the clanking of chains. The sense of touch may also come into it, as when a cold draught causes shivers down the spine or cobwebs drift across the observer's face. A ghost is commonly understood to be a phantasm produced in some way by the spirit of a dead person. This is not, however, necessarily so. There have been ghostly horses, ghostly carriages (but not so far ghostly motor-cars) and spectral wolves and dogs, as in the hound of the Baskervilles, although this was not only fiction but a fake ghost as well.

Belief in ghosts goes back to the beginning of history and has been claimed to have been concerned with the origins of religion. But although there is justification for a belief in there being two aspects of a person, the body and the spirit (that is, the ghost), the very idea that the spirit can possess a material existence and can restlessly prowl about the derelict house in which its corporeal life was spent, banging doors and moaning, must be, by the definition of the spirit, a fallacy.

Ghosts and apparitions can be of several sorts. There are those which are frankly bogus and produced by trickery. There are others

which arise, often in a dim light and under circumstances when the observers are keyed up or frightened, from the misinterpretation of natural objects. There is a report of a number of ghostly children having been seen leading a ghostly horse. This, on closer examination, turned out to have been two men carrying beehives suspended on a pole. A historical example was Sir Walter Scott's vision of the ghost of Byron, lately dead. When Scott looked into the matter more thoroughly he found that what he had seen had been a collection of plaids and cloaks hanging in the hall at Abbotsford. Another type of ghost can be the result of hallucination. Hallucination can arise from insanity and other morbid conditions of the brain and nervous system, or from drugs or drink. Pink elephants are less common than popular belief would imply, but ghosts can arise as the result of alcoholism. Hallucinations can also come to people who are suggestible and can occur in the borderland between sleeping and waking.

Although statistical evidence is notoriously lacking, it would appear that the number of ghosts actively haunting in modern times is dwindling to the point when such apparitions could be said to constitute an endangered species. There may be several reasons for this. Whether or not the increase in common sense is one, the spread of electric light and improved housing, diminishing the number of dark, creaking mansions, the doors of which are opened by cadaverous old butlers, may have had something to do with it. Changed attitudes to the nature of the human spirit – or soul – together with advances in the understanding of the biochemical mechanism of the living body may be another. While too strong a belief in the material aspect of life is to be deplored, recognition of the fallaciousness of spooks and ghosts haunting the monastery cloisters with eerie shrieks and rattling chains (or even, at times, with their heads tucked underneath their arms) is all to the good.

HYPERKINESIS

In 1973, Dr Ben Feingold, an American physician specializing in the treatment of allergies, brought to public attention a new children's disease called 'hyperkinesis'. You know, it seems, if your child has got it if he or she is (a) restless and more active than other kids, (b) does not concentrate for long on any particular activity, (c) acts on impulse, (d) hates to be balked whenever he or she wants something and (e) is troublesome both at home and at school. It must be admitted that this is a curious disease, if disease it is, because to the jaundiced eye – and the Americans do admit that there are sceptics in communities outside America – its symptoms sound remarkably like the sort of behaviour with which large numbers of ordinary mothers, fathers and teachers had to deal before the disease was invented.

American parents are more inclined to take hyperkinesis seriously because they tend to take children more seriously than non-American parents do and because, if hyperkinesis exists, they need not blame themselves if they fail to keep their children in order at home and if the children bring home bad reports from school, should the truth be that they are not naughty but ill. Before one would dare to say that the notion of hyperkinesis is a fallacy rather than a disease, one must try to decide what a disease is. Shakespeare talks about 'life's fitful fever', implying that every activity is a sickness. We can hardly go as far as this. Yet, discussing hyperkinesis, a contributor to the Annals of the New York Academy of Science, admits that it calls for special clarification in 'the murky realm of nosology'. (Nosology is the classification of diseases.)

This fallacy, however, if it *is* a fallacy, has another fascinating ramification. Dr Feingold is not only convinced that he knows where the normal, healthy restlessness of childhood ends and hyperkinesis begins, but he also claims to know how the disease can be cured. This, he states, is achieved by omitting almonds, apples, apricots, berries, cherries, currants, grapes, raisins, nectarines, oranges, peaches, plums, prunes, tomatoes and cucumbers from the child's diet and specially cooking all foods from ingredients known to be free from artificial colours and flavours. He is particularly insistent that the whole family should be involved in the operation to make sure that there is no chance of the hyperkinetic child getting hold of forbidden fruit or coloured or flavoured items. Using this regime, Dr Feingold claimed dramatic successes, with children doing better at school and being less troublesome at home.

Naturally, the medical profession in America was interested in these claims but anxious to be sure that it was the diet that caused the changes in behaviour rather than the general disturbance of the home and the attention being paid by anxious parents going to so much trouble on behalf of the children. A series of studies was, therefore, set up in six different parts of the States, two in Canada and one in Australia. Large numbers of allegedly hyperkinetic children were given the Feingold diet to which, without the knowledge of either the experimenters, the children or their families, various of the prohibited articles were added. The children's behaviour was measured in all sorts of ways. In one test, for example, a chair was wired up so as to record on a chart exactly how much the child sitting in it fidgeted over a test period. The degree of hyperkinesis was also judged by the parents, by the children's teachers and by the researchers. After five years of work, the results were reviewed by a National Advisory Committee comprising representatives of the American Medical Association, the Mayo Clinic, the Food Safety Council, the National Institute of Health and half a dozen of America's leading universities. Their final conclusions were that the idea of any connection between hyperkinesis, the components of the foods itemized by Dr Feingold and artificial colours and flavours, was a fallacy. They did not, however, express an opinion about the reality of hyperkinesis itself.

L

LAETRILE

A current fallacy which is still enjoying a vigorous lease of life in the United States is that amygdalin, a substance extracted from the stones in apricots, can be used as an effective treatment for cancer. Many pips and stones in common fruits contain substances like amygdalin, which are compounds of cyanide. There is, indeed, a report in scientific literature of a man who liked the taste of apple pips. One year he collected an eggcupful and on his birthday he ate the lot and died of cyanide poisoning. Under ordinary circumstances, the amounts of cyanide are not very large and what the cyanide-containing substances contribute to the good life is merely a flavour reminiscent of bitter almonds. In 1951, however, an apricot-stone extract appeared on the market in America under the designation 'Laetrile'; that was the name concocted by a certain Ernst Krebs, Junior, as a contraction of what purported to be its main chemical component, *Laevo-amino-nitrile*-beta-glucuronic acid. And this was the substance which, quite without proof, was claimed to cure cancer. The rationale underlying the claim was that cyanide gradually released from it would kill cancer cells while leaving healthy cells unaffected. The fact that there was no evidence that Laetrile did, in fact, exert any effect, good or bad, on cancer cells did not deter those who soon began to make money selling Laetrile to desperate people who believed in its effectiveness.

To start with, the Federal Food and Drug Administration, backed up by the State of California and one or two other organizations whose business it was to protect American citizens against fallacious claims by people battening on their fears, particularly of cancer, initiated a number of prosecutions. But then in the mid-1960s, the Laetrile people floated a new fallacy. They renamed Laetrile and transmogrified it into 'Vitamin B_{17}'. Of course, Laetrile is not a vitamin. It is hard to understand how anyone could have been persuaded to believe that it was. Vitamins are minor components of food, lacking which an experimental animal or a person will develop recognizable symptoms of deficiency. This is not so with Laetrile. Nor is there any evidence that cancer is a vitamin-deficiency disease. At the same time, however, those interested in the commercial side of Laetrile were able to take advantage of the more liberal regulations controlling the sale of vitamins compared with those covering drugs.

The propagation of belief in Laetrile forms a striking example of the power and subtlety of fallacy. Cancer is a deeply feared disease of which more and more people can expect to die in view of the fact that it tends to be, in the main, a disease of later life and, because of the successes of medicine, fewer people die young, so inevitably more die older. It would be deeply comforting, therefore, if the claims for Laetrile were true. It thus follows that those promoting its use through an organization designated The Committee for the Freedom of Choice in Cancer Therapy speak with a persuasive voice. By 1978, it was estimated that 75,000 Americans had resorted to Laetrile, regardless of the fact that no rational evidence was available of its effectiveness while every effort by the National Cancer Institute to organize trials of its *bona fides* had been circumvented. By this date also, seventeen of the United States had placed laws accepting Laetrile on their statute books.

Here we have then an example of the potency of fallacy. The deeply ingrained philosophy of the United States is a belief in the sanctity of what its citizens see as the free capitalist ethic, whether it is in the distribution of hand-guns as a preventative of violence, or of Laetrile as a preventative of cancer, regardless of any rational assessment of the effectiveness of either. In the Soviet Union, the national philosophy is different. There they believe in the supremacy and wisdom of the state. In the decade succeeding World War II, the community accepted, not an unproved remedy for cancer, but an unproved method for increasing the yield of crops, disregarding the evidence of genetics, hard won by science since the time of Mendel. In due course, the fallacy of Lysenko purporting to offer a short cut to the increase of crop yields in the USSR became apparent, but not before Soviet science had been hampered for a generation. The fallacy of Laetrile is still to be exposed as is the damage it may inflict on serious scientific researches into the mechanism and treatment of cancer.

'LET THEM EAT CAKE'

There is much to be said in favour of Marie Antoinette, the unfortunate Queen of France who was executed during the French Revolution. At the end, she faced her accusers and eventually went to her death with great dignity and courage. Yet today, two hundred years later, should one stop that popular entity, the man in the street, even if such a man (or woman) can lay claim to a tolerable education, all that he will know – or think he knows – with any certainty is that, being told that her people had no bread, the Queen callously coined the phrase by which she is still remembered: 'Let them eat cake.'

Here then we see, in a particularly damaging form, the melancholy result of accepting a fallacy. Still, long after Marie Antoinette's enemies have left the political scene, we find unthinking people believing in her coldheartedness. Yet it is now known that she did not originate the saying attributed to her. The phrase was used, in Latin, by John Peckham, Archbishop of Canterbury, in the thirteenth century; it was attributed to Marie Thérèse, wife of King Louis XIV, who died in 1683, in the form 'why don't they eat pastry?'; while Rousseau in his *Confessions*, written in 1740, fifteen years before Marie Antoinette was born, quotes it as a well-known saying.

Whether Marie Antoinette ever used the phrase at all is doubtful. What is undoubtedly a fallacy is the belief that it was she who made it up.

LEVITATION

It really is remarkable what people will believe and for how long over the years other people will continue to believe the same unbelievable fallacy. The belief in levitation, for example, which is the power to raise the human body up into the air by occult

means, is ancient and widespread. The blatant fallacy of such belief has certainly been swallowed by credulous people from the fourth century AD until the nineteenth century, and one may safely prophesy that any time now some enterprising newspaper reporter will come up with an account of a barmaid in darkest Yorkshire or a gypsy in Cornwall claiming to be able to rise up into the air at will. And his million readers will believe him. The well-known public house trick whereby four men put two fingers behind the elbows and knees of a fifth seated in a chair and cause him to rise into the air is sometimes peddled as an example of the occult.

It should, of course, be said that it is common for stage magicians to include levitation as an item in their repertoire. But that is a different thing altogether. We know, if we are sensible, that this is a trick. The fallacy which I am now describing is that for fifteen centuries or more there were those who believed that levitation could really occur, and some gullible people will still believe it today.

The Indian rope trick (in which a rope is thrown upwards into the sky and held there by magical force so that a boy can climb up it and disappear into the air) is, one could say, a variant of levitation which, in the days of Kipling, could still muster its believers. In the ancient writings, the *Puranus*, there is, in Sanskrit, a description of 'the preternatural power of making oneself lighter at will', while the Buddhist *Suttas* describe a similar power. Then there was an account that 'the enthusiastic disciples of Iamblichus (who died at Chalcis in Greece in about AD 333) affirmed that when he prayed he was raised to the height of ten cubits (that is about 15 feet) from the ground'.

Moving forward by thirteen hundred years or so, we come in the seventeenth century to Joseph of Cupertino, a Franciscan monk, of whom it was said that 'frequently he would be raised from his feet and remain suspended in the air'. The report then continues: 'Since such occurrences in public caused much admiration and disturbance . . . Joseph for thirty-five years was not allowed to attend choir, but was ordered to remain in his room and say his prayers on his own.'

The limits of human credulity are, it would appear, boundless. Not only must we accept that devout men in ancient India, that

Greeks of the fourth century and monks of the seventeenth century, in ages before the rationalism of scientific thinking had begun to show people something of the mechanism of the natural universe, could believe the fallacy of the suspension of the laws of physics, but we must also accept that scientists themselves can be fooled. In December 1868, a certain Mr Daniel Home agreed to demonstrate before witnesses his ability to raise himself off the floor in his London house. After having put himself into what was assumed to be a trance, he rose up into the air, floated out of the window, which was seventy feet from the ground, and floated back in through another window seven feet from the first. Sir William Crookes, a distinguished Fellow of the Royal Society, wrote an account of the whole incident which he published in the *Quarterly Journal of Science* for January 1874 and was quite convinced of the genuineness of what he had seen.

The lesson once again must be learnt. In the rational world we inhabit, 156lb bodies do not rise up and stay suspended in mid-air. It is a fallacy to believe that they do. And if a conjurer convinces us that we have seen a woman sawn in half, a set of table spoons miraculously bent, or a Mr Home floating unsupported out of the window, we must try to retain enough common sense to be aware that what we have seen is a clever trick, regardless of the number of university professors who have allowed themselves to be deceived.

LIE DETECTOR

What is commonly called a 'lie detector' or 'polygraph' is an instrument which records readings of the pulse rate, the blood pressure and the moisture of the palm of the hand of the individual being tested. Useful information can be derived from these readings, but it is, perhaps, a fallacy to assume that a lie detector of this sort will infallibly indicate when the person under test is telling a lie. It is true that the heart of a man or woman under stress will beat faster. It is also true that his or her blood pressure may rise. Candidates waiting to learn the result of their application for a passionately desired appointment can feel the thump, thump, thump of their hearts as the chairman of the appointments board clears his throat prior to making the fateful announcement. It is also true that under conditions of stress, apprehension or fear, the palms of the hands of a man or woman will sweat. There is a sound physiological basis for the popular expression 'sweating it out'.

To operate a lie detector, the forensic scientist applies electrodes to the person under test to time the heart rate, tightens a cuff to his or her upper arm to measure blood pressure, and tapes other electrodes to the palm of one hand to assess moisture by means of electrical conductivity. The instrument is then switched on, and a series of pens begins to draw the base lines across a steadily unrolling strip of paper ruled with cross markings to indicate the elapse of time. The interrogation then begins. Perhaps to check the validity of the readings and the skill of the operator, a special preliminary test may be set up. For example, the person under examination may have been required to conceal some valued object in a particular room on a selected floor of a building. If during his questioning aimed to discover, against the will of the person under test, where the object has been secreted, the operator is able to observe a series of peaks in the recordings when he is becoming 'warm' – as children put it – he knows that the physiological responses of the subject under test are giving him away. A great deal depends, however, on the skill of the questioner, but even more depends on the self-control of the individual being tested. It has been found that there are those with sufficient strength of mind to be able to suppress their reactions and tell lies without influencing the recordings of their pulse rate, blood pressure or the moisture of their palms. Good poker players could be expected to excel at this exercise. It could thus be said that the lie detector cannot of itself be claimed to detect lies. Perhaps it is better called a polygraph, meaning merely that it is an instrument that draws many lines. It could, however, be of use, if he was permitted to use it, to a juryman trying with his naked eye to assess the veracity of a prisoner in the dock, or to an employer attempting to judge the reliability of an applicant for a job, each of whom try to detect whether those under scrutiny are pale, flushed or whose hands sweat when asked tough questions.

LINDBERGH

The achievements of Charles Lindbergh as an aviator stand on their own merits. On 10 May 1927 he left San Diego for New York, his flight establishing a record. On 20 May 1927, flying alone, he left New York and, to the admiration of the world, safely arrived in Paris. In December of the same year, he flew non-stop from Washington DC to Mexico City from whence he flew 7860 miles through South America and the Caribbean.

These remarkable achievements stimulated the admiration of the press, whose words, as sometimes happens when great events are afoot, generated a fallacious impression which has lasted ever since. This is that Lindbergh was the first man to cross the Atlantic by air. In fact, the first transatlantic flight was made by Lieutenant-Commander A. C. Read and his US Navy crew in 1919 from Newfoundland to England. The second flight was made in the same year by two Englishmen, Captain John Alcock and Lieutenant Arthur Brown from Newfoundland to Ireland. The third flight, also in 1919, was carried out by Major G. C. Scott and his crew in the airship R34 from Scotland to New York and back to England. In 1924, during a round-the-world flight by US Army aeronauts, the Atlantic was crossed from Europe via Iceland and Greenland, and in the same year a German airship under the command of Dr Hugo Eckener flew from Friedrichshaven to New Jersey. In 1926, Commander Franco flew from Spain to Argentina. In 1927, Commander de Pinedo flew from Italy to America and back. Only then did Lindbergh make his flight to Paris.

There is an ancient saying that if a tree falls in the desert where there is no one to hear it, it falls without a sound. On the basis of this reasoning, one could argue that, since no one was there to record its existence, the tree was not there either. Those people who write history books, or for that matter write newspaper columns or work at radio or television stations, tend to believe not only that the events they do not record do not happen, but they also believe – as do the people who read or hear their words – that what they describe as being the true record of events is, in fact, the truth. But it may be a fallacy. Because so much was written and spoken about

Lindbergh, it did not make him the first man to fly the Atlantic. That was Lieutenant-Commander Read, regardless of the fact that his name has long been forgotten. Because the literate civilized world knew little and wrote less about the Norse voyagers who were probably the first Europeans to discover the continent of America, Christopher Columbus has had the credit ever since, even though the land he sighted in 1492 was one of the islands of the Bahamas. It surely does take a cool head and all the knowledge one can acquire to avoid fallacy.

LOCH NESS MONSTER

There is something so reassuring and appealing about 'Nessie' that in this case, more than most, it almost hurts to turn the harsh light of scientific reason on the monster which has kept us all happily guessing for over half a century, and which presumably must be doing its fair share for the Highlands and Islands tourist drive.

It is only right to point out, though, that in spite of its best endeavours, the Loch Ness Phenomenon Investigation Bureau has failed to come up with any conclusive proof of the monster's existence. It would be comforting to think of the beastie lurking beneath the murky waters of the loch, having a private chuckle and giving us all the occasional tantalizing glimpse of a humped back – or was it a head, a flipper, or a fin? However, on the other side of the scale comes the convincing argument put forward by a leading zoologist, Dr T. E. Thompson of Bristol University, which pours the cold water of scientific reasoning on our wild imaginings. Dr Thompson's thesis appears in full in Mr Philip Ward's *A Dictionary of Common Fallacies II* (The Oleander Press, 1980). Here I merely outline his arguments against the existence of the monster.

Dr Thompson begins by pointing out that the very limited number of sightings of the monster argues against there being 'a sizeable number of individuals' of the quantity required for a stable breeding population. Furthermore, as 'Nessie' is invariably depicted as a

large aquatic reptile, one would expect far more sightings, since reptiles, particularly large ones, 'must breathe air at the surface'.

Lastly he tackles the question of how the monster came to be in Loch Ness in the first place, bearing in mind 'that the loch must have been frozen during the recent geological past'. He dismisses the idea of underground channels connecting the loch with the sea, since the loch would drain to sea-level if these did indeed exist. The freshwater connection too is inadequate 'to submerge even a small monster', he argues. While the idea of the monster arriving at the shores of the loch by land has to be ruled out because such a trip 'would be impossible for an aquatic vertebrate of the size and specialization claimed'.

Until something more concrete can be fished out of the waters of the loch, I'm afraid that Dr Thompson's arguments against 'Nessie' look horribly convincing.

MEDICAL FALLACIES

Doctors very often find themselves in a difficult position. Their speciality has two aspects. One is the art of healing, the other the science of medicine. Great things have been achieved, almost entirely within the present century, by medical science. For example, within our own lifetime medical discoveries, starting with the heroic – and highly dangerous – eighteenth century vaccination with smallpox virus, followed by Jenner's virtually safe cowpox vaccination (a major step forward in medical knowledge) has now led to the extermination of smallpox from the face of the earth. This is a shining example of the scientific understanding by which doctors can heal their patients (and without which they cannot) or, better still, protect them from becoming ill in the first place. But while modern medical science gives doctors power over many of the ills of the flesh which afflicted our grandparents, for example, pneumonia, typhoid, cholera, malaria, poliomyelitis, diabetes, pernicious anaemia and much more, it is not complete. The art of healing leaves the doctor doing the best he or she can for an individual patient when medical science is incomplete. Yet the speed at which medical science has advanced, the fact that many of the diseases due to bacterial infection can already be controlled, that there is reason to expect that virus diseases will soon be controlled too, that degenerative ailments such as kidney disease, Parkinsonism and arthritis are yielding to scientific research, that cancer and heart disease may follow, and that surgery accepts virtually no limits to its versatility – all this has led to the first dangerous fallacy about medicine.

(1) *The fallacy of the omnipotence of modern medicine* It is a fallacy to believe that because no one suffers from smallpox any more, every human ill is equally preventable. Medicine can do much but not everything. We all have to die and – what is now sometimes forgotten – no matter how long the medical scientists may delay our terminal illnesses, we all have to die of something.

(2) *Homoeopathy* It is, perhaps, unfair to blame the German physician, S. C. F. Hahnemann, for having based his system of homoeopathic medicine on a fallacy when one bears in mind that when he propounded it in 1796 much of orthodox medicine lacked any rational basis as well. The first principle of homoeopathy was that 'like should be cured by like'. This idea is borrowed from the very much older 'doctrine of signatures', which, in spite of its antiquity, is fallacious nevertheless. Because beetroot, or port wine, is red, it does not follow, as the 'doctrine of signatures' would imply, that beetroot or port is good for the blood. Hahnemann's modification of this doctrine was that the drugs he used should produce, when tested on healthy people, symptoms similar to those of the diseases they were intended to cure. A second principle of the homoeopathic system was the use of extremely small doses of the various drugs recommended. But regardless of the efficacy of these drugs and the dosages employed, there was a strong spiritual, as distinct from rational or scientific, aspect in homoeopathic medicine. 'It is only by means of the spiritual influence of the morbific agent', wrote Hahnemann in his book *Organon*, 'that our spiritual vital powers can be diseased, and in like manner only by the spiritual operation of medicine can health be restored'.

When homoeopathic treatment was introduced at the end of the eighteenth century it was of benefit to many of the patients of its practitioners, not because of the peculiar choice of drugs designed to produce the symptoms they were intended to cure but because so little of them was used. In those days, two hundred years ago, not only were some of the drugs – mercury, for example – used in orthodox medicine harmful in the excessive doses in which they were employed, but also some of the treatments – phlebotomy (bleeding) was one – were harmful as well. Under these circumstances, a system which effected virtually nothing could well constitute a medical benefit.

Today, when the majority of medical scientists consider that to believe in the efficacy of homoeopathic drugs and methods is a fallacy, note that even those who still cling to the spirituality of homoeopathy prudently assert as part of their doctrine that 'a homoeopathic physician is one who adds to his knowledge of medicine a special knowledge of homoeopathic therapeutics'.

(3) *Chiropractic medicine* This is a system based on the fallacious premise that all disease is caused by some sort of interference with nerve function. It was devised by an American, Daniel David Palmer, in 1895. By 1903, he had achieved sufficient success to be able to establish the Palmer School of Chiropractic in Davenport, Iowa. By the middle of the present century, there were schools of chiropractic scattered over the United States and extending into Canada.

The basic notion of chiropractic therapeutics, that disease is caused by malfunctioning of nerves, was linked to a second equally unsubstantiated generalization that all other systems and physiological processes of the human body are controlled and coordinated by the nervous system. Basing their practice on these two premises, the chiropractitioners set out to restore normal nerve function – regardless of whether the patient was suffering from gout, cirrhosis of the liver or Bright's disease – by manipulation and treatment of selected structures of the body, especially those of the spinal column.

Here again, as with homoeopathy, we have people in substantial numbers pinning their faith on a system of medicine for which the rational basis is weak and the safe application limited. But a further point is that it can be argued that both these beliefs spring from the first fallacy into which many patients, and sometimes one or two doctors as well, may fall. In the United States, where belief in science is sometimes less critical than it is elsewhere, legal actions against doctors and hospitals are common because of the general, and fallacious, belief that every sickness is amenable to modern scientific medicine. Thus, when some patients discover that, great though the achievements of science may be, pain, disability and even death still hold sway, they may blind themselves to what scientific knowledge *has* achieved and embrace some unorthodox system based in whole or in part on fallacy.

(4) *Faith healing* Faith healing goes back to times of antiquity. Cures were claimed for the rituals in the temples of Aesculapius and other gods in distant pagan days; the practice of being touched by the king – the Lord's anointed – from the eleventh to the eighteenth century as a cure for the 'king's evil', scrofula (a chronic swelling of the glands); and attempts to cure disease by magical rituals of

all sorts, are examples of faith healing. When no effective remedy for a particular disease was known, it was not surprising that people should put their faith in relics, exorcism and in the power of whatever healer should come along. In the seventeenth century, there was Valentine Greatrakes, the 'stroker'; throughout history there have been holy relics and rituals alleged to possess therapeutic efficacy. Towards the end of the nineteenth and the beginning of the twentieth century, as science began to change medical practice, although most of the effective drugs which have revolutionized our outlook on sickness were still to come, there was a sudden flood of faith healing, belief in which continues to some degree to this day.

Christian Science, for instance, holds that pain is an illusion and seeks to cure the patient by instilling into him or her this belief. Pain is, indeed, a subtle phenomenon. In the heat of battle, men can fight on feeling no pain even though afflicted by horrific wounds. Nevertheless, it is a fallacy to presume that a sufferer from a burst appendix will gain much benefit from 'thinking himself' free from pain: unless he puts himself into the hands of an orthodox physician, he will die.

Christian Science was invented by an American lady, Mrs Mary Baker Eddy. When, by taking thought, she brought about her own recovery from an injury, it came into her mind to initiate a 'scientific system of divine healing'. By 1875, Mrs Eddy had published the first edition of her main book, *Science and Health*, which, following the later establishment of the Church of Christ Scientist, was read at services side by side with the Bible. The most distinctive feature of Christian Science teaching is its absolute distinction between what is real and what is unreal. And what are unreal, according to this doctrine, are sin, disease and death. Presumably, those who have sufficient faith in this gospel will not become ill and, should they do so, will be able to convince themselves of the unreality of their diseases.

The system of alleged self-healing developed by Emile Coué in 1910 in Nancy in France could be argued to lie on the frontier between fallacy and truth. Undoubtedly there are a number of illnesses in which the mind plays a part. So long as Coué's system of psycho-therapeutics was restricted to those conditions possessing a psychosomatic content, some good could be achieved, as with other sorts of faith-healing. Where fallacy arose was in the assumption that it was applicable to diseases which, as is now known, call for other forms of treatment. The peculiarity of the Coué system was that it did not depend on the administrations of any charismatic healer using the 'laying on of hands' or the touching of magic relics. Coué emphasized that he was not himself a healer but that he taught people who were sick to heal themselves. His best known formula was to persuade patients to repeat over and over again, 'Every day in every way, I am getting better and better', until they believed it.

(5) *The fallacy of absolute safety* A modern fallacy widely held by members of the general public, and by newspaper writers and broadcasters who aim to reflect their views, is that drugs and vaccines can be made to be absolutely safe. More than this, it is assumed that drugs should be demonstrated to be absolutely safe before being permitted to be offered for sale to the public or for prescription by doctors. A minute's reflection makes it clear that the possibility of attaining absolute safety is a fallacy.

Aspirin is now well established as a safe painkiller. Yet it is well known that the consumption of a bottleful of aspirin tablets at one go can be fatal. Insulin is a potent remedy, by the use of which diabetics, who would otherwise die, can live a normal life – but of which an overdose can bring disaster. These points are commonly overlooked when, in the proper search for a sensible standard of safety, members of the public and their legislators demand an unattainable level of safety. This fallacy is a particularly damaging one when it leads, as is happening now, to the blocking of the search for new and better medicaments because, no matter how stringently they may be tested before coming into use, there will always be some level of danger, maybe forty years on, in their application. Thus no scientist, doctor or pharmaceutical manufacturer can ever hope to obtain a certificate of approval from those adherent to the fallacy of absolute safety.

MIRROR – bad luck to break

Although it is a fallacy to believe that bad luck and misfortune must necessarily fall on anyone who breaks, or even cracks, a looking glass, the fallacy possesses ancient and respectable antecedents. Today the rational evidence of science tells us that life is a biochemical mechanism. The energy that keeps life going is derived from the combustible fuel we consume as food. If part of the mechanism of a living body breaks down, the kidneys, for example, or even the heart, we know how to keep the life-process going while we replace the defective part. In our clear understanding of how life works there is no place for a belief in any such ill-defined entity as a soul. People differ from each other in virtue, character and ability, we now understand, because of the differences in their DNA, the deoxyribose-nucleic-acid, the chemical molecule of heredity. In the past, when none of this current scientific knowledge had been discovered and more people than now had first-hand experience of death, whereby the body of an active, living man in a moment gave up the ghost, perhaps at the hands of the executioner, and fell down, an insensate lump of flesh, they found it reasonable to believe that a man or woman was made up of two kinds of stuff: body and soul. They could also rationally believe that a man's shadow and, more particularly, his reflection in a glass, was in some way a part of his soul. They would naturally conclude that if the mirror cracked and broke, the soul itself would be injured and misfortune ensue. We are not quite sure today what kind of thing our soul is, but we know that it is not harmed when a mirror breaks.

MOON – effect on human behaviour

Here is a letter published in the *Journal of the Royal Society of Medicine* on 25 November 1982 from the Professor of Environmental Health, School of Public Health, University of Sao Paulo, Brazil:

'Dear Sir, In a recent paper, Pollitt stated that "lunar cycles could explain the lunacy and monthly mood changes said to occur in man and in animals". This would confirm the general popular belief that the lunar cycle can affect human behaviour.

'If the lunar cycle does affect the behaviour and mood of humans, it could also be responsible for a greater number of accidents at work due to personal factors which, as is well known, are sometimes implicated in 80 per cent of such accidents. In an attempt to prove or disprove this hypothesis, a study was carried out to relate this type of accident to the lunar cycle.

'A total of 3024 consecutive cases of accidents at work occurring in the industrial undertakings of Sao Paulo were studied, and the day of their occurrence distributed according to the phases of the moon (Table 1). Using the X^2 distribution at the level of significance of 0.01, the calculated X^2 was 3.17 and the critic X^2 was 11.345. These results therefore show clearly that there is no relationship whatever between the phases of the moon and possible factors which could lead workers to behave differently and, consequently, to be more prone to accidents of occupational origin.

'The study suggests that normal human beings are not affected by the lunar cycle. Yours sincerely, D. P. Nogueira.'

Table 1. Number of accidents at work according to the phases of the moon on the day of their occurrence.

New moon	975 (25%)
First quarter	973 (25%)
Full moon	957 (24%)
Third quarter	1019 (26%)

In the United States, considerable attention has been paid to beliefs in the postulated influence of the moon on human behaviour. A study was carried out in Miami claiming to link murders with the phases of the moon. Subsequent work, however, failed to substantiate any such relationship. Similar researches were carried out in Cincinnati on the dates when most crimes were committed which again failed to demonstrate any relationship with the lunar cycle. In Texas, whereas three tests appeared to relate insanity to the phases of the moon, 45 other tests showed no evidence of any connection. Other studies failed to relate the date on which people committed suicide with the state of the moon.

Because in the dark days of superstition, people believed in werewolves, howling and drinking the blood of their victims at full moon, it seems perverse that people should still cling to the tattered remains of the fallacy that madness, murder, suicide and crime are influenced by how much of the earth's shadow falls on the moon.

MUSTARD GAS

It could be argued that it is a fallacy to describe mustard gas as a gas because, at ordinary atmospheric temperatures, it is a liquid. In fact when, during World War I, it was used, it was the droplets of dichloro-diethyl-sulphide, to give it its scientific name, falling on the soldiers' skin which did most of the damage. There the chemical caused severe blisters and burns: and because mustard 'gas' is a very stable liquid, its potential for doing harm and causing injury persisted for days or weeks in any area where it had been released.

All liquids, whether water, petrol or, for that matter, mercury or mustard gas, release a certain amount of gas at whatever temperature they may be held. It is reasonable to describe sea water as a liquid, even though it exists in balance with the water vapour which it is always releasing. The amount of water vapour around us exerts a considerable influence. For example, we experience clammy humid weather when there is a lot of water vapour in the atmosphere, and bracing, stimulating weather when there is only a little. Yet we still rightly describe water as a liquid. Of course, if we lived at a temperature higher than 212°F (100°C), water could no longer be described as a liquid. We should have to designate it a vapour or gas – or just call it steam.

The same principles apply to mustard gas. Even though those who breathe a sufficient quantity of its vapour (or gas) will suffer from inflammation of the lungs, it does exist in the main as a liquid at ordinary atmospheric temperature. If we wished to be strictly accurate, therefore, we ought to call it mustard liquid. Accurate speech is an admirable target for those who believe it is important to think clearly and avoid fallacy. Perhaps, however, those who want to continue to call dichloro-diethyl-sulphide mustard gas may be forgiven for doing so, provided that they know it mainly exists under normal circumstances as a liquid.

NERO

Those who concur in the statement that the Emperor Nero fiddled while Rome burned involve themselves in two kinds of fallacy. To start with, the violin, of which 'fiddle' is a popular colloquialism, was not invented until 1579, whereas the reign of Nero extended from AD 54 to 68 and the fire, at which the fiddling was alleged to have taken place, occurred in AD 64, fifteen hundred and fifteen years before there were any fiddles.

The question as to whether it was a fiddle that Nero is supposed to have played or some other instrument is, however, of less importance than whether Nero was in fact sufficiently unfeeling as to amuse himself with music of any sort during the disaster in which a large part of the capital city of his empire was destroyed. The type of fallacy which each one of us today must constantly take pains to avoid is that in which we find ourselves believing the slanders and rumours put about by the media, by political opponents and all sorts of other interested parties to blacken the names of public figures. I have already pointed out that Marie Antoinette did not coin the phrase about eating cake and it is doubtful whether she ever used the expression at all. In the case of Nero, the position is made more doubtful by virtue of the fact that he was particularly unpopular at the time of the fire. But let us see what Edward Gibbon had to say about it.

'In the tenth year of the reign of Nero', he wrote, 'the capital of the empire was afflicted by a fire which raged beyond the memory and example of former ages. The monuments of Grecian art and of Roman virtue, the trophies of the Punic and Gallic wars, the most holy temples, and the most splendid palaces were involved in one common destruction. Of the fourteen regions or quarters into which Rome was divided, four only subsisted entire, three were levelled to the ground, and the remaining seven, which had experienced the fury of the flames, displayed a melancholy prospect of ruin and desolation.'

Gibbon then continued: 'The vigilance of government appears not to have neglected any of the precautions which might alleviate the sense of so dreadful a calamity. The Imperial gardens were thrown open to the distressed multitude, temporary buildings were erected for their accommodation, and a plentiful supply of corn and provisions was distributed at a very moderate rate.' Surely this does not seem like unfeeling behaviour? Gibbon's narrative, however, continues thus: 'But all the prudence and humanity affected by Nero on this occasion were insufficient to preserve him

from the popular suspicions . . . The voice of rumour accused the emperor as the incendiary on his own capital; and, as the most incredible stories are the best adapted to the genius of an enraged people, it was gravely reported, and finally believed, that Nero, enjoying the calamity which he had occasioned, amused himself with singing to his lyre the destruction of ancient Troy.'

Even today it may appear that 'the most incredible stories' may still be accepted, if not by an enraged, at least by an unthinking people who thereby involve themselves in fallacy.

NUMERICAL FALLACIES

Numbers and all the remarkable manipulations to which they can be subjected have fascinated mankind since the dawn of history. They possess their own characteristics yet, at the same time, it has also been the divine reasoning of the human mind which has brought to light the seemingly magical properties relating music and mathematics and the movements of the stars. It is, therefore, little wonder that, regardless of the rational nature of mathematics, fallacies have developed about numbers.

I have already referred to the irrational beliefs which people have in lucky numbers. The equally unreasonable belief in the unluckiness of the number 13 is still so strong that I have given it an entry to itself.

There are those who accept such fallacies as that the date of their birthdays is a particularly lucky number. Then again, as recently as the 1930s, there was a vogue superstitiously asserting that a number derived from the letters of one's name could be either lucky or unlucky. The system was operated thus. From the name JOHN SMITH, of the two vowels, O is the 15th letter of the alphabet and $1+5$ scores 6, while I is the ninth letter of the alphabet and scores 9. The two, added together, come to 15 which, in the obscure rules of the system, gives an overall score for the two vowels of $1+5$, namely 6. The consonants by the same system of scoring come to $1+8+5+9+4+2+8$, that is 37, which as $3+7$ or 10 scores as 1. The sum of the vowels and the consonants therefore comes to 7. Having reached this point – the numerical representation of his name – the adherent to this extraordinary belief looks up in a list, originally derived, it is said, from Cornelius Agrippa, to see whether a person named JOHN SMITH whose name has the number 7 is 'unimaginative', 'pessimistic' or 'lacking in versatility', or, on the other hand, 'practical', 'of high endurance' or 'assured of material success'. It is said that those who believe in this rigmarole of numerical nonsense actually select their spouses and the names of their children and, more bizarre still, change their own names by deed poll in order to ensure themselves of an appropriate numeral.

Dr Wilhelm Fliess, who was a contemporary of Freud in Vienna, conceived a numerical fallacy based on the belief that people's lives were governed by two rhythmic cycles, one of 23 days and the other of 28 days. He purported to show that these cycles could be demonstrated by changes in the mucous lining of the nose. Freud, who was initially convinced by Fliess' hypothesis, expected to die at the age of 51, this being the sum of 23 and 28. Long before he actually did die, at the age of 83, he had lost faith in Fliess.

Recently Fliess' ideas have acquired a new lease of life in the United States by the popularization of a pseudoscience called 'biorhythms'. This is based on the idea that each person is influenced throughout life by three (not two) rhythms, starting on the day of his birth and continuing to the day of his death. The first is a physical cycle of 23 days, the second an emotional cycle of 28 days and the third an intellectual cycle of 33 days. Success in athletics, love and intellectual achievement is better assured when the appropriate rhythm is high rather than when it is low. The bible of the believers in biorhythms is a book *Is This Your Day?* by a Mr George Thommen, of which many thousands have been sold. The curves of rising and falling rhythms are conveniently calculated with a special electronic calculator, the Biolator, currently available for $30, while computer print-outs can be obtained for a further modest charge. Unfortunately, when submitted to rigorous tests, the hypothesis on which the system is claimed to function did not hold up. Star baseball and golf performers were no more successful on days predicted by their biorhythms than on any other days, nor did people die more often when their rhythms were low. Equally unsuccessful were the attempts by young mothers to forecast the sex of their imminent babies by the use of the appropriate highs and lows as claimed by the rules of biorhythms. It can confidently be deduced that the claims of the pseudoscience of biorhythms are as fallacious as were those of Fliess from whence they were derived.

Numerical fallacies can arise from incomplete understanding of the rules of mathematics, quite apart from mistaken observance of the mucous lining of the nose. Here, for example, is a so-called proof that $+1$ can equal -1.

$$\frac{+1}{-1} = \frac{-1}{+1}$$

It therefore follows that $\dfrac{\sqrt{+1}}{\sqrt{-1}} = \dfrac{\sqrt{-1}}{\sqrt{+1}}$

Multiplying both sides of the equation by $\sqrt{-1}$, we obtain

$$\sqrt{+1} = \sqrt{-1} \times \sqrt{-1}$$

Since $\sqrt{+1}$ is $+1$ and $\sqrt{-1} \times \sqrt{-1}$ is -1 we reach the fallacious conclusion that $+1 = -1$.

A different numerical fallacy can be obtained by dividing by zero. Assume that $A + B = C$ and that, let us say, $A = 3$ and $B = 2$. If we multiply both sides of the equation by $A + B$ we obtain

$$A^2 + 2AB + B^2 = C(A + B)$$

This can be rearranged thus

$$A^2 + AB - AC = -AB - B^2 + BC$$

If we then prepare to divide both sides of the equation by $A + B - C$ we obtain

$$A(A + B - C) = -B(A + B - C)$$

This implies that $A = -B$ or, on the other hand, that $A + B = 0$ which is nonsense because $3 + 2$ is not 0.

How guarded must the rational citizen be to escape the error of fallacy, when it can be seen that even the cold logic of mathematics can be twisted to deceive the unwary.

OSTRICHES

It is, perhaps, forgivable to believe that ostriches, when threatened by their enemies, bury their heads in the sand, believing, poor foolish birds that they are, that because *they* cannot see their attackers, their attackers cannot see *them*. This notion has been common currency for a very long time. It was, for example, given respectability by Pliny in the first century AD in Book X of his writings. Nevertheless, it is a fallacy.

Flightless birds, of which the ostrich is one, have had a hard time in this cruel and ruthless world. The dodo did not stand a chance. It did perfectly well in Mauritius and Reunion until these islands were discovered by Western explorers. Then the dodo was doomed. In spite of the fact that the flesh of the dodo, no matter how it was cooked, had a disgusting taste, the sailors killed dodos for fun. The last pair was slaughtered in 1681.

Most of the flightless birds of New Zealand were destroyed, either by men or by such other introduced species as dogs, cats or rats.

The ostrich of Arabia and Africa, the biggest and, in the opinion of some people, the ugliest living bird on earth survived partly because of its inedibility, partly because of its capacity to defend itself by striking out with its feet, but mainly because of its speed. If only some of those people who so innocently accepted the fable about its burying its head in the sand had used their wits to think about the matter for themselves, they would have come to a healthier state of scepticism. So foolish a habit on the part of the ungainly flightless ostrich would have been seen not to be compatible with its survival.

★

PALMISTRY

Because a fallacious belief is old, it does not follow that it is any the less a fallacy. Neither does it follow that because people in large numbers continue to give credence to an untenable hypothesis, this makes it any the more true so long as it is not supported by evidence of its truth.

Palmistry, by which it is supposed that the mental and moral characteristics of an individual, as well as the future events in his or her life, can be deduced from the irregularities and folds of the skin of his or her hand, was practised in China 3000 years BC. In Greek literature, even in the most ancient writings, palmistry is treated as a well-established belief. Today it is still widely practised even in communist China, in Syria, Egypt and other Arab countries.

Over the years, palmistry has acquired a formal set of rules although they are not always the same in different parts of the world. The line separating the ball of the thumb from the rest of the hand is the 'line of life'. Another line is the 'line of the head'. A transverse line crossing the palm is the 'line of the heart'; another is the 'line of fortune', and so on. Then again, the protuberance at the base of the thumb is the 'mountain of Venus', that at the base of the index finger is the 'mountain of Jupiter', and further along are the 'mountains of the Sun, the Moon, Mercury and Mars'.

The idea that these purely mechanical aspects of the structure of the hand, some of which are influenced by manual work, possess any predictive meaning related to the future behaviour and prosperity for the individual whose hand it is, is quite beyond the reach of reason. It is paradoxical that members of an educated community which demand rigorous evidence of the safety of innovations in motor cars and the effectiveness of drugs can still be found to accept the farrago of improbability in palmistry, quite unsupported by evidence.

★

PARAPSYCHOLOGY

As someone who is prepared to stand up and be counted, I am prepared to classify parapsychology, together with its offshoots, clairvoyance, extra-sensory perception (ESP), telepathy, precognition and psychokinesis, as fallacies. I shall be quite prepared at any time to think otherwise should the various groups of people involved in diverse aspects of psychic research eventually prove able to provide hard evidence for their reality. Meanwhile, however, I find such evidence as is put forward in their support unconvincing.

Parapsychology, defined as those allegedly supernormal capacities of the human mind which I have listed above, has had its believers all over the world in ancient times when the potency of spells and curses, witches and the evil eye was widely accepted. In its modern form, however, parapsychology first owed such acceptance as it has won, as a branch of psychology, if not of science, to J. B. Rhine in America in 1934, even though his work attracted serious criticism. In brief, to show that someone possessed the power of clairvoyance – that is to say, the ability to see something not visible to the normal eye – Rhine used a special pack of five cards bearing the symbols of a cross, a circle, a star, a square and a wavy line. If, after these were dealt face down on the table, the examinee could correctly guess more cards than could have been expected by chance, it was assumed that he or she possessed clairvoyant powers. A number of variants of this procedure were followed and from time to time clairvoyant powers were claimed for particular individuals. The results, however, were not particularly convincing, nor were the alleged clairvoyants thus discovered able to see through anything more than the backs of playing cards.

Similar experiments were also done to demonstrate telepathy, the transmission of thought at a distance. These tests required two people. One looked at a card or other object and the other attempted to receive the thoughts which the first projected towards him to tell him what the card or object was. Sometimes the sender and the receiver were in the same room, sometimes they were stationed further apart in different rooms. But whatever the arrangement, the results again were not particularly impressive.

Precognition is the rather grand name for the ability to foresee what is going to happen in the future. In attempts to demonstrate precognition under scientific conditions, Rhine and his collaborators asked those under test to forecast the order in which cards would be dealt from a pack or numbers thrown from a dice. Again the results were unconvincing – which was probably just as well for the proprietors of gambling clubs!

In 1938, the American Psychological Association (not, be it noted, the parapsychologists) canvassed 603 of their members. Of these, 2 per cent considered parapsychology an established fact, 7 per cent thought it a likely possibility, 36 per cent believed it to be a remote possibility, 15 per cent considered parapsychology and all its offshoots totally impossible, while the remaining 40 per cent were prepared to allow that they knew nothing about it.

Regardless of the doubtful successes achieved by investigators of the 1930s in establishing the existence of extra-sensory perception, researchers in America and elsewhere persevere. Making use of a German technique from fifty years ago, the *Ganzfeld* technique, they cover the eyes of those subjected to the studies, put earphones over their ears through which noises of the sea, the countryside, soft music or instruction can be transmitted and, when they have attained a sufficiently complete state of disorientation, ask them to say whatever comes into their heads. At the end of the session, those people subjected to all this are asked to pick one out of three or four pictures, in the hope that they will select the one at which the researcher has been gazing. If they do, this is taken as an example of thought transference. More recently, finding that telepathy (reading another's thoughts in this manner) and clairvoyance (perceiving a distant scene) are difficult to demonstrate with any reasonable degree of statistical certainty, some American workers have taken to using video games as tools. The idea is that people showing particular talent in playing Space Invaders and the like, may possess paranormal abilities in foreseeing where on the screen a space ship is likely to appear.

Appreciating the weakness of the evidence supporting the very existence of parapsychology and the whole rigmarole of so-called PSI phenomena, researchers in the field have sometimes argued that the very presence of investigators in white coats and the use of electroencephalographs and other scientific instruments may be inimical to the functioning of parapsychological activity. Of course, another argument is that if the phenomena cannot be demonstrated to exist by rational experimentation, the whole thing is a fallacy.

Of all the branches of parapsychology, perhaps psychokinesis has been the most troublesome to demonstrate under laboratory conditions. Psychokinesis (PK), the ability to make physical things happen by the direct influence of thought waves, has often been used in the admittedly fictional context of horror movies. In the more modest surroundings of a research laboratory, researchers have used a video game in which the players attempt to steer the image of a motor car through a maze of random dots which appear as the game proceeds. It is hoped that players possessing PK powers will be able to influence the machine so that the random dots do not impede the car's progress across the screen.

There are plenty of theories about how the different aspects of parapsychology *might* work; there are serious researchers carrying out studies by diverse techniques, there are even larger numbers of people who feel in their bones that there must be *something* in PSI. There are many more, I hope, who consider it more reasonable to reject the unbelievable as fallacy until there is good evidence to demonstrate the contrary.

PERPETUAL MOTION

The story of perpetual motion is a good example of the harm which can arise from believing in fallacies. It is a lovely idea to imagine that one can construct a machine capable of producing a perpetual supply of energy without the use of expensive fuel. One would become rich and one's country prosperous. But supposing that it cannot be done, that the idea is a fallacy, what then? Gradually, the wretched inventor loses heart, he spends all his money on constructing models. He pursues his friends – or his bank manager – for loans. He sees large sums of capital provided on his advice by credulous (or greedy) investors being frittered away. If he is honest but misguided, he ends up a frustrated and disappointed bankrupt, which is bad. But if he is unscrupulous – and some of the fallacies already described in this book have been products of dishonesty – he may stoop to deception and launch as genuine what he knows to be bogus, which is worse.

The idea that something could be got from nothing by means of a perpetual-motion machine is as old as Archimedes, but practical efforts to construct such a machine were not seriously started until the seventeenth century when Robert Fludd, an English physician, taking note of the large number of water-mills to be found grinding corn, sawing wood, grinding pigments to make paint, processing wool and tanning leather all over the country, wherever there was a stream to work them, planned to do something for the people who had no water flowing on their land. His thinking was that if the water that turned the mill-wheel could be collected from the mill-race below the wheel and somehow put back into the reservoir up above, a self-contained perpetual-motion mill would result which could be installed anywhere. Centuries of experience had shown (the Domesday Book recorded in the eleventh century 5600 water-wheels in operation in England) that mill-wheels could turn big grind-stones and raise heavy hammers. Why, then, could the wheel not pump up its own water supply?

Another early device was demonstrated to King Charles I in 1640 by the Marquess of Worcester. This was a wheel, 14 feet in diameter, fitted with forty loose hammers with 50lb heads. As the wheel turned, one by one, each hammer over-balanced with a bang which, it was claimed, would keep the wheel turning for ever. Later, a whole series of variations of this idea were constructed, some with balls rolling down channels in the curved spokes of the wheel, others with weights on chains fixed round the wheel, more complicated ones with floats in tanks attached round the circumference. None of them worked.

Over the years, hopeful inventors have tried a variety of systems other than overbalanced wheels and water-mills designed to do work *and* to pump up the water to drive themselves. In the 1670s, John Wilkins, Bishop of Chester, who was concerned with the early administration of the Royal Society, a wholly respectable scientific institution, gave a good deal of thought to perpetual motion. Having exhausted the more direct approach, he designed a system whereby a magnet pulled an iron ball up a ramp. Just before the ball would have reached the top of the ramp where the magnet was, it dropped through a hole, ran back down a second ramp, popped through a door and emerged at its starting point at the bottom of the first ramp where, if the system had performed as planned, the magnet would have pulled it up again. Ingenious though this seemed, it did not work either. Sir William Congreve designed another ingenious device working on quite a different principle. In this, weighted chains pressed unequally on a series of sponges which were pulled out of a tank of water. The idea was that on the side where the sponges were dripping wet, they would be heavier than after they had been squashed by the pressure of the chains. I need hardly say that this system was as ineffective as all the others.

There are two ways in which scientists 'prove' that perpetual motion is a fallacy which sensible (and honest) people should usefully avoid. The first is to refer to experience, namely, that no one has ever been able to demonstrate its possibility. This type of argument, though frequently sufficient – after all, in spite of Joshua getting the sun and the moon to stand still, so far as practical astronomy is concerned, these bodies can be depended upon to keep moving – it has its dangers. Karl Popper, the philosopher, has, for example, referred to the mythical scientist who, over a period of forty years had examined several thousand swans and reached the conclusion that all swans are white. It was on his seventieth birthday that he first came across a black swan. The second proof of the impossibility of perpetual motion is that it would be contrary to the First Law of Thermodynamics. This law states, among other things, that energy can neither be created nor destroyed. If a perpetual-motion machine were to do work, it would need to create energy over and above the initial energy put into it to start it. For the eager inventor, who is often no scientist, the problem with the First Law of Thermodynamics is that the evidence upon which it is based is subtle and diverse and by no means easy even for a scientist to grasp, let alone a layman. I would, however, advise such laymen to accept the fact that it is, so far, firmly established on the statute book of truth.

Now let us see what damage the reluctance to accept truth and the
greediness to embrace fallacy by people in general does by giving
scoundrels the opportunity to pretend that fallacy is truth. By the
time that the Laws of Thermodynamics had shown those who
understood them that perpetual motion was impossible, there came
in 1813 one Charles Redheffer of Philadelphia to display publicly
(for money) 'incontestably a perpetual self-moving principle'. The
main part of this machine was a big gear-wheel driven by a little
pinion. Before long, however, it was discovered that Mr Redheffer's
machine was driven by a hidden clock spring. Another machine
with weights sliding on inclined planes was exhibited in New York.
A sceptical onlooker who knocked away some light wooden sup-
ports purporting to steady the machine exposed a catgut belt drive
which led to an old man in the attic turning a crank.

About fifty years later, John E. W. Keely launched a 'hydro-
pneumatic pulsating vacu-engine' for the promotion of which he
sold shares on the market in the million-dollar Keely Motor
Company. These were eagerly taken up. The design comprised a
generator coupled to a motor. The generator was a complicated
structure of pipes and valves, metal globes, nozzles and gauges.
After blowing into a nozzle, Keely would pour in five gallons of tap
water which after a while he claimed to have been converted into
'inter atomic ether' by a vibrator which formed part of the appara-
tus. Keely asserted – and people believed him – that his machine
would derive enough energy from a gallon of water to take a ship
across the Atlantic. The machine was later shown to be a fraud and
to have been run by compressed air carried in concealed pipes.
Belief in such a fallacy, however, demonstrated a failure to understand that the Second Law of Thermodynamics cannot be broken
any more than can the First. The Second Law broadly states that
hot gases or, for that matter any other hot things, when left to themselves, get cooler. You cannot expect them to go the other way and
become hotter.

The story of Mr John Gamgee and the 'zeromotor' is perhaps
the most remarkable example, not this time of outright cheating,
but of the fallacy of people believing the unbelievable. Gamgee's
machine was not unlike a normal steam engine except that, in order
to avoid the necessity to use fuel to produce steam to run it, it was

designed to work at the freezing point of water, namely 0°C. But instead of using water as its working fluid, it used ammonia. Since ammonia boils at −33°C, Gamgee argued that the heat of the environment would vaporize the ammonia to give a pressure of 4 atmospheres. This would work the pistons. His idea was that when the ammonia vapour then expanded, it would turn back into liquid and drain back into the reservoir from which it came, where it would be ready for further use. This, of course, was a fallacy. To get the ammonia vapour to liquefy it would either have to be compressed (when the machine would not work), or it would need to be cooled to −33°C. Such a cooling process would require refrigeration equipment demanding more power than that delivered by the 'zeromotor' itself. The grotesque feature of all this was not only that Mr Gamgee, from the depth of his ignorance of the Second Law of Thermodynamics, convinced himself that the 'zeromotor' would work, but that Mr B. F. Isherwood, Chief Engineer of the US Navy, reported favourably on it to the Secretary of the Navy. He arranged for members of the Cabinet to inspect a model of the 'zeromotor', after which the US Cabinet, worried by the expense of maintaining coaling stations all over the world, recommended President Garfield to consider substituting the thermal energy of sea water, as harnessed by the 'zeromotor', for coal as an energy source to run the American Navy. This was no distant fallacy of superstitious antiquity; it happened in 1881.

But this was not the end. The French Academy of Sciences may, quite rightly, have refused to consider any further communications on perpetual motion as long ago as 1775, nor will the US Patent Office accept patent applications based on perpetual motion. Yet the charlatans persist, the ordinary citizens hope. After I showed the fallacies of half a dozen devices on TV in 1980, I was deluged with further impossible designs submitted by hopeful inventors – the crackpots persist. In 1918 an expert commission was set up by the US Congress to investigate a proposition put forward by a gentleman called Garabed Giragossian to supply America with free energy. His invention was, in fact, the fly-wheel. He had observed that a fly-wheel, brought up to speed by a 1/20th horsepower motor, delivered 10 measured horsepower when its brake brought it to a stop. Neither Mr Giragossian nor the congressmen, it seems, had grasped the difference between energy and power, nor realized that to rank as perpetual motion, the motion of a machine must continue for ever, and during all that time provide something for nothing. Common sense, quite apart from the First and Second Laws of Thermodynamics, tells us that in this world, as a wise American once said, there is no free lunch.

PHARAOH'S CURSE

It was after the tomb of Tutankhamun was opened and its rich appurtenances displayed to the world that the ridiculous fallacy was circulated, by people who should have known better as well as by those concerned with popularizing horror movies, that anyone involved in the desecration of the Pharaoh's grave would be cursed.

When Lord Caernarvon died in his hotel bedroom on 5 April 1923, six weeks after the tomb was opened, the superstition gained its initial momentum. Shortly afterwards, Georges Bénédite, Head of the Department of Egyptian Antiquities at the Louvre in Paris, also died. Credulous people were happy to attribute his death to the alleged curse, even though he died of a stroke. When later on A. C. Mace, Assistant Keeper of the Department of Egyptian Antiquities at the Metropolitan Museum of Art in New York, who had taken part in the Tutankhamun excavations, died, the fear of a supernatural spell was strengthened among the gullible.

From then on, the death of anyone remotely connected with the opening of the tomb was taken as evidence of malevolent occult powers. Not only was the curse assumed to have caused the death of Robert Bethnell, the one-time secretary of the expedition's leader, but also to have brought about the demise of Bethnell's father, Lord Westbury, at the age of seventy-eight. By 1935, twenty-one deaths had been attributed by credulous believers to the curse of the Pharaohs, even though Howard Carter, the discoverer of the tomb, the expedition's photographer, the doctor who had carried out the autopsy of the mummy, and Sir Alan Gardner, who was present when the tomb was opened, were all alive.

PHRENOLOGY

Phrenology is an old fallacy but an account of its rise and fall is instructive nevertheless. It was a piece of pseudo-science invented by an expert and, as such, provides a solemn warning to us today. Experts are valuable people in their own field but when they stray into other areas of knowledge and, worse still, when they construct what purport to be scientific systems out of their own heads unsupported by hard evidence, they are as susceptible to error as anybody else. The moral for the ordinary citizen is, in examining scientific hypotheses, to use the same sort of common sense as he or she does when trying to ferret out the truth as a member of a jury.

Phrenology was a system developed in 1800 by a German anatomist called Franz Joseph Gall. Noting that certain parts of the brain control certain functions of the body, somehow or other he got the idea that the shape of the brain could be used as an indicator, not only of the intellectual abilities of the person it belonged to, but also the personality of the individual concerned. That is to say, it could indicate whether he or she was jolly and kindly; dishonest and addicted to crime; musical; taciturn; or good at languages. Gall's second notion, as fallacious as the first, was that the shape of the brain was reflected in the shape of the skull. Phrenologists who accepted these ideas believed that by a careful examination of a patient's skull they could assess his or her personality and abilities. As a boy, I well remember the consulting rooms of practitioners of phrenology who discreetly advertised their services by placing in the window a life-sized plaster head, the scalp of which was painted with lines indicating the personality traits alleged to be found in that part of the brain lying beneath. Gradually, as the fatuity of the system slowly became apparent, the cult of phrenology died away, much as did a parallel belief in palmistry.

There seem to be fashions in fallacies just as there are for anything else. Today we have flying saucers and men from outer space. At the end of the eighteenth and the beginning of the nineteenth century, fallacies derived from anatomy were popular. Almost at the same time that Gall, in Germany, was inventing phrenology, a Swiss, Kaspar Lavater, was developing physiognomy. This also

was a so-called science purporting to enable its adherents to read a person's character from the shape of his or her features. A striking indication of the potential harm which the belief in fallacies may cause is shown by the fact that Captain Fitzroy, the commander of HMS *Beagle*, proposed to oppose the appointment of Charles

Darwin as biologist to the very survey expedition which enabled Darwin to collect the knowledge on which his discovery of the origin of species was based. Fitzroy's opposition was based on the grounds that, according to the rules of physiognomy, the shape of Darwin's nose indicated that he was unsuited for the job! Luckily, Fitzroy overcame his doubts and came later to accept that Darwin's nose had spoken falsely.

POPULATION EXPLOSION

Although the world's population has been increasing quite rapidly over the last two or three generations, it is a fallacy to believe in a population *explosion*. Babies are not fired from guns like puffed rice. For the most part, parents have children because they want to.

The world's population may legitimately be divided into two unequal parts, the rich and the poor – or, as the current jargon has it, the developed and the developing – in which numbers increase at two different rates. It is, however, arrogant for those who belong to the rich and educated section (who are likely to read this book) to assume that those who are less wealthy and who live in tropical parts of Africa, Asia and South America have their children, not because they love them any less than do those who are rich, white and technologically advanced, but because of some explosive force. Above all, it is a fallacy to assume that this alleged explosion of poor children is going to blow the world to pieces.

It is true that a number of unimaginative demographers have forecast alarming population increases, but already these are being shown to be mistaken. In the mid-1970s, about one-third of the world's population lived in Europe, North America, Australia, favoured parts of South America and were rich (like we are). On average, 1000 women in these places gave birth to 1300 baby girls, of whom about 50 died before they could grow up and become women. It thus followed that in a generation there were about 25 per cent more women than there had been in their mothers' time.

This implies, since a generation is about 25 years, a population increase of 1 per cent a year. In poor countries, however, 1000 women were at the same time giving birth to 2800 little girls of whom 840 died, leaving something fewer than 2000 to grow up into the next generation. This represented an increase in the population of 2.6 per cent a year.

But because in one generation it is common for there to be between 4 and 6 children, of whom 2 to 3 are girls, in the family, it does not follow that these children will themselves have as big families when they grow up. There are several reasons why they should not. In England and Wales there was a dramatic fall in the size of people's families between 1875 and the end of the century. It is easy to say that this must have been due to the advance in technology and the prosperity which technology brings. It can now be seen, however, that this only partly explains what happened. When the industrial revolution began, the population dramatically increased with the new opportunities which became available. There was – had our current misleading phrase been invented then – a 'population explosion'. The fall in family numbers which later began to occur in 1875 did have something to do with wealth and prosperity, yet the odd thing was that it took place equally in the poorer parts of the country as well as in the more prosperous ones. What happened was that people living in depressed areas *heard about* the way richer people were reducing the size of their families and did the same.

A striking example of the way in which, by taking thought and quite apart from the use of scientific contraceptives, people may choose as free agents to reduce the number of children they have is the modern history of the province of Quebec in Canada. When I was a student there in the 1930s, the French Canadians, who were mainly Catholics, had large families, while the mainly Protestant English-speaking Quebecois mostly had small families. By the 1970s, when I was again in Canada, the number of children in the families of the French-speaking Canadians (who were still Catholic) were on average fewer than that of their English-speaking neighbours. The irrelevance of whether communities are Catholic or not and whether they employ contraceptive devices or not (although these may play their part) compared with the way the people think and feel and, having thought, exercise their free will, is strikingly shown in the Republic of Ireland where there has been little or no increase in the population for the last hundred years or more because men choose to marry late.

Today, when apprehensions about a so-called 'population explosion' are most widespread, opinions and attitudes can be communicated widely and at greater speed than ever before. The notion that family numbers can be limited by direct governmental intervention has been proved to be unsound ever since Moses as a baby was hidden in the bulrushes. There are still areas of domestic activity into which government inspectors cannot properly penetrate. On the other hand, when the citizen has changed his or her mind, the time lag between the recognition by him or her of the advisability of planning a small family and the implementation of the plan can be greatly reduced.

A striking illustration of the speed at which population increase may be reduced once its members have decided that they want it to be so is the island of Mauritius. There the average number of children per family fell from 5.4 in 1966 to 3.0 in 1973, a reduction of 45 per cent in seven years. This gave an average family containing only one and a half girls, which thus shows no evidence of an 'explosion' in a 'developing' society. The changes in West Malaysia, although less dramatic, have been of a similar kind. In the late 1950s, the average number of children for Malayan mothers was about 6, while the Chinese and Indians in the mixed community had 7 or more children. Within twenty years, all three ethnic groups raised families all with an average of slightly fewer than 5 children. This represented a steady drop of about 25 per cent.

Demography, the statistical study of the factors affecting population numbers, is of all disciplines the most inexact. This is because it attempts to deal with, among other things, what people are likely to feel and do in the future. Populations increase in numbers at different speeds and such increases (or decreases) may change abruptly. Who could have predicted that the possession of transistorized radio sets, wrist-watches and motor-cars would have ranked so high in the catalogue of human desires as to influence the fertility of nations! Equally, the density of population can seem desirable or undesirable for what appear to be unaccountable reasons. The great crowded cities of the eastern seaboard of the United States, Hong Kong, Singapore and Tokyo in Asia are among the richest places on earth. Crowding is a matter of taste. There are nearly 60 million people in the British Isles. In the fertile, temperate acres of New Zealand, which has an area of similar size, there are only 3 million people. 'What do you consider would be the ideal population for New Zealand?' I asked a friend when I was there. 'Three million', he said.

The human race has, during its history, encountered disasters of various sorts, yet it possesses a self-correcting mechanism by which an equilibrium – even if an unstable one – is re-established. The notion, therefore, of an irreversible 'population explosion' seems to me to be shown by the evidence to be a fallacy.

PORCUPINES

There is a well-established fallacy that when porcupines are attacked by an enemy, they turn their backs and fire quills at their pursuer. In spite of the difficulty which the porcupine would find in aiming when in this posture, belief in its abilities has been steadily maintained even though no clear idea exists of what sort of mechanism would be required to project the quills towards their target. Is it suggested that each quill is flipped on its way by a sudden muscular contraction, comparable with the way a boy fires a paper pellet with an elastic band? Or is it thought that pressure developed within the animal shoots off a quill as from a water pistol? Fortunately, there is no need to speculate, since the whole idea is a fallacy.

The true facts are clearly stated by Dr P. A. Racey of the Department of Zoology of Aberdeen University, who found it necessary to reprove the London *Times*, no less, for having propagated the porcupine fallacy.

'Permit me', wrote Dr Racey to the editor of the newspaper on 14 October 1982, 'to correct an error which appeared in *The Times* of 5 October that porcupines shoot their quills'. And he went on,

'No mammal has yet evolved such a defence. When cornered, porcupines back up to an enemy and flick their tails. Their quills are only loosely embedded in their skin and easily become detached when they make contact with the enemy. Such is the ease of detachment that loose quills may be thrown some distance by the tail flick, which is presumably how the myth of shooting quills originated.'

PYRAMIDOLOGY

Pyramids, the royal tombs which were developed in Egypt and achieved their most impressive stage in 4700 BC, are among the most remarkable structures built by man. It is, therefore, particularly sad that there should have accrued around them a penumbra of fallacious nonsense which has persisted to the present time. Indeed, today's beliefs – for example, that safety-razor blades positioned in a pyramid retain their sharpness – are among the most trivial and foolish of all those which have attested to the credulity of man throughout history, and this up to a period which prides itself on its knowledge and understanding of the world.

The most remarkable of the pyramids is that of Cheops (Khufu), which stands at Gizeh, 480 feet high, second only to the Great Wall of China, as the most massive structure ever built. It was erected nearly five millennia before Christ. This pyramid excited the wonder of the Greeks and the Romans and was used by Napoleon as a fixed point for the mapping of Egypt by his engineers. Then in 1859 John Taylor, no scholar but a member of a London printing firm, a man who had never seen the great pyramid at Gizeh but merely made use of measurements made by a Colonel Howard Vyse who had broken into the interior in 1829, wrote what became a best seller. This was a book called *The Great Pyramid: why it was built and who built it*. It was this work which started the fallacies that the builders of the pyramid had been gifted with supernatural powers enabling them to foresee the future.

To start with, Taylor pointed out that the height of the pyramid divided by twice the length of the side of the base equalled *pi*, the relationship between the diameter of a circle and its circumference. He also claimed that the builders of the pyramid had used in their mensuration the biblical cubit. This led him, by a process of thought in which reason played no part, to the conclusion that the actual builder must have been Noah, who had received his instructions on how to do so direct from God. This was the start of pyramidology.

Among those who attached weight to Taylor's book, lacking in sensible observation though it was, was Charles Smyth, a Fellow of the Royal Society and Astronomer Royal for Scotland. The fact that he gave credence to Taylor's intrinsically unbelievable speculations is a warning to ordinary citizens that, although they can justifiably attend to what scholars may say about the subjects in which they are qualified to express an opinion, such scholars may be as gullible as anybody else on topics in which their opinion is no more valuable than yours or mine. Like Taylor, Smyth wrote a popular book, *Our Inheritance in the Great Pyramid*, without ever having seen it. Later on, however, he did go to Egypt, where he spent four years making numerous measurements of the structure. Having considered the figures he obtained, he deduced (1) that the pyramid was laid out in 'pyramid inches', each of which was one twenty-fifth of the width of the stones in which it was encased, (2) that the length of the base of the pyramid divided by the width of one of these stones came to 365, the number of days in a year (this calculation was subsequently found to be inaccurate), (3) that the width of a casing stone must be (for no particular reason) the *cubit* used by Noah in building the ark, Abraham in building the tabernacle and Solomon in building the temple. He also calculated (4) that the height of the pyramid multiplied by 270,000 was equal to the circumference of the earth and (5) that the length of the side of the pyramid multiplied by 1,000,000,000 was equal to the distance of the earth from the sun, and much else of equal irrelevance.

By measuring off distances between corners and side-passages inside the pyramid in 'pyramid inches', starting at a point representing the creation of the earth, as calculated by biblical students if not by the paleontologists of the day, as 4004 BC, Smyth purported to show that the pyramid builders had foretold not only the year 1486 BC, the date when the Children of Israel set off from Egypt at the exodus, but also – this was the work of later disciples of Smyth – the date of World War I, the great depression of 1930, the second coming of Christ in 1874 (this one they must have got wrong), and 16 September 1936, the date when King Edward VIII announced to Stanley Baldwin that he proposed to abdicate from the throne of Great Britain to marry Mrs Simpson.

One would have imagined that this collection of fallacies based on the assumption of the magical nature of the pyramid's construction would have sunk under the weight of its intrinsic improbability. In the 1970s, however, claims for the existence of 'pyramid power' were made by a Czech radio engineer, Karel Drbal. He did not use the giant pyramid of Gizeh to demonstrate his thesis, but obtained his results with model pyramids made out of cardboard and other material more easily managed than limestone blocks. These models, however, conformed broadly to the proportions of the Gizeh pyramid. Drbal claimed that razor blades, appropriately orientated and situated at one-third the height of the pyramid, retained their sharpness and food retained its freshness for two weeks. Even though no serious evidence has been adduced to substantiate his claims, and trials carried out in Canada failed to do so, people are still to be found who are prepared to spend money to purchase cardboard pyramids sharing, it is implied, the allegedly supernatural qualities of the Great Pyramid of Cheops in Gizeh, while manufacturers are happy to sell them.

RATS – deserting ships

There can be no more disheartening sight to the hapless sailor than to be cruising along one minute with everything shipshape and secure and to have the decks swarming with rats leaping over the side the next.

According to the popular fallacy, though, this is just what will happen. Rats, it holds, are gifted with some intuitive foreknowledge of disaster which leads them to desert otherwise sound and seaworthy craft.

Well-meaning investigators have tried to explain this old wives' tale in logical terms. They picture a sinking wreck, its hold awash, the rats' nests submerged and the homeless rodents making a bid for safety as they evacuate the bilges. Unfortunately this ignores the crucial issue, that the rats are supposed to leave otherwise intact vessels. The rat of popular belief is a treacherous creature, not one responding to an obvious calamity.

The truth of the matter is that there is no way of proving that rats did or did not desert the numbers of ships that have suddenly gone to the bottom either as the result of an explosion, sabotage or freaks of climate, disasters unforeseen by the crew. From the widespread use of rats in laboratory tests, no evidence has come to light suggesting that they are blessed with any greater prescience than you or I, and neither of us I trust would take it unto ourselves to leap suddenly over the side of the QE2 for no apparent reason.

RED RAG TO A BULL

It is a widespread popular fallacy that bulls become enraged and excited by the colour red. People believe that if they are compelled to cross a field with a bull in it, they should wear any colour other than red and that, when faced by a group of intruders in his field, a bull will charge the one wearing red. Based on this fallacy, innumerable seaside postcards have been printed depicting fat ladies wearing red underclothes being hotly pursued by enraged bulls,

and red-nosed men confronted by bulls with lowered horns pawing the ground with their feet. In fact, a bull is no more excited by a rag because it is red than by one of any other colour. Bulls, in common with cattle in general, are colour-blind.

Bull-fighting dates back to ancient Thessaly in Greece and became a popular spectacle in imperial Rome. Its particular connection with Spain arose from the fact that in that country a special breed of peculiarly ferocious bulls was developed which gave better sport than domesticated animals which, while they do occasionally attack people, only rarely do so.

By the year AD 45, Roman writers were already referring to the use by Spanish bull-fighters of skins or cloaks to confuse and tire the bull, but there was no reference to their being red, rather than any other colour. It was long afterwards, in about 1700, when bull-fighting had become a complex, stylized – if dangerous – dance, that the great matador, Francisco Romero from Andalusia, introduced the *mulita*, the red worsted cape folded over a short stick. The colour, red, was chosen not to stimulate the bull, but to support the pride of the man. Red concealed better than other colours any stains, and particularly any stains of blood, should the bull, contrary to the intentions of the bull-fight manager, succeed in wounding the man in one of the exchanges of the contest.

RHINOCEROS HORN

The damage which belief in fallacy can do is strikingly shown by the sufferings of the poor, strange, harmless rhinoceros. This curious beast, a perissodactyl mammal, wrapped up in its armoured skin, seems so palpably a leftover from a prehistoric age. Surely, no one would want to do it any harm, even if the books of reference do describe rhinoceroses as 'large, massively built animals, with little intelligence and a bad temper'. And even if their sight is dull, their hearing and their sense of smell are acute. Once upon a time, in the Miocene and Pliocene periods, they roamed about both in the eastern hemisphere and in the Americas. Now we are left with the Indian rhinoceros in Assam; the Javan rhinoceros in Java, Sumatra and Borneo and in Burma and Bengal; the black rhinoceros south of Abyssinia, and the white rhinoceros in Zululand and the Upper Nile. Once there was a woolly rhinoceros living in Europe but it became extinct. How much longer will its successors survive?

These strange creatures, by whose presence the earth is enriched, are victims of a widely held fallacy. Millions of men believe that its horn (which is not a horn at all, that is a fallacy too – it is made of modified hair) when powdered up and eaten acts as an aphrodisiac. This makes it a powerful lure for poachers, who pursue this innocuous vegetarian beast to its death, to cut off its horn for money. Within a decade, so it is forecast, all the rhinoceroses in the world may be exterminated, except for those few kept alive in zoos or nature reserves. And for what? There is no evidence that powdered rhinoceros horn has any effect, either good or bad, on the sexual performance of those who consume it. The idea that it has is a fallacy.

RICE PAPER

Rice paper can quite legitimately be described as paper but it is not made from rice. The fallacy of believing that it is is of long standing. The fact that it came originally from China, where people eat rice, may have had something to do with it.

Rice paper, being thin and delicate and obviously different from the ordinary paper with which Europeans were familiar, led to those who had no real knowledge of its manufacture jumping to the conclusion that it must be made somehow or other from rice. A slightly more substantial reason why this error continued for so long (and indeed persists to this day) is because it is used as a backing for the flat cakes called macaroons, made out of ground almonds, egg white and sugar. Because the rice paper stuck tenaciously on to the bottom of the macaroons and consequently had to be eaten, rather than being removed as is ordinary paper put under cakes when they are being baked, the idea became confirmed that, being erroneously thought to be made from rice, it was edible. In fact, the Chinese make the paper from a cylindrical core of pithy wood from the trunk of a small tree, *Aralia papyrifera*, found growing in swampy land mainly in Formosa, now Taiwan. The workmen adjust a sharp knife against the revolving cylinder and shave a continuous strip of the 'rice' paper. Apart from what is needed for macaroons and other industrial purposes, most of it is coloured and employed to make artificial flowers.

ST SWITHIN'S DAY

The notion that if it rains on 15 July, St Swithin's Day, it will rain for the subsequent forty days, is a particularly English fallacy. No one expects it to operate in Saudi Arabia or Alice Springs. The myth originated in AD 981. In that year, on 15 July, the monks of the cathedral at Winchester decided to remove the remains of St Swithin from the churchyard and re-inter them inside the cathedral. This sacrilegious act was, it appears, followed by forty days of continuous rain.

Since meteorological records have become available, no record has occurred of forty days of continuous rain whether or not it rained on 15 July. Indeed, this part of the summer in England has been found to be somewhat drier than average. Yet there are people who still cling to the fallacy of St Swithin.

SHROUD OF TURIN

The so-called Shroud of Turin is an ancient piece of linen, 4.4 metres long and 1.1 metres wide, on which can be seen the faint images of the front and back of a man bearing the marks of the scourging and crucifixion suffered by Christ as described in the Gospel. It was first reported as being exhibited for money in about 1357 at Lirey in France as the genuine shroud in which Christ had been wrapped when put into the tomb thirteen centuries before. As soon as he heard about it, Bishop Henri de Poitiers denounced the shroud as a hoax and brought this enterprising method of raising money to a stop. Thirty years later, however, the local ecclesiastical authorities started again to exhibit the shroud. This stimulated Bishop de Poitier's successor, Bishop Pierre d'Arcis, in 1389, to write to Pope

Clement VII begging that he bring to an end 'the contempt brought upon the Church' and the 'danger to souls'.

'The case, Holy Father', he went on, 'stands thus. Some time since, in the diocese of Troyes, the Dean of a certain collegiate church, to wit, that of Lirey, falsely and deceitfully, being consumed by the passion of avarice and not from any motive of devotion but only of gain, procured for his church a certain cloth cunningly painted . . . Many theologians and other wise persons [were sceptical] that this could be the real shroud of our Lord, having the Saviour's likeness thus imprinted upon it, since the holy Gospel made no mention of any such imprint, while if it had been true, it was quite unlikely that the holy Evangelists would have omitted to record it, as that the fact should have remained hidden until the present time. Eventually, after diligent inquiry and examination, he (Bishop de Poitiers) discovered the fraud and how the said cloth had been cunningly painted, the truth being attested by the artist who had painted it, to wit, that it was a work of human skill and not miraculously wrought or bestowed.'

It could be imagined that this strong statement would have put a stop to this example of fallacy, and so it would appear to have done from the fourteenth to the twentieth century. Today, however, in this very age in which the use of reason, as exemplified by science, has given us the material benefits we see all around us and the powers, upon which we so pride ourselves, we see a widespread upsurge of fallacy. This is particularly apparent in America, where science and its application have advanced most vigorously. In 1978, thirty American scientists, carrying with them more than six tons of sophisticated equipment, spent five days in Turin examining the shroud. At about the same time the Shroud of Turin Research Project (and how could it avoid being called STURP?) was set up. Unfortunately, these scientists fell foul of the principle which, if they were to avoid fallacy, is as important for scientists as for anybody else, namely, *Occam's razor*. Broadly speaking, what William of Occam was saying in 1340 was that the fewer explanations suffice to elucidate a problem the better. On this occasion one might say that if the STURP scientists had restricted their researches to the determination of traces of iron to be detected in the pigments forming the image on the shroud, they would have been better advised than to concur – as they did – with the postulate that a burst of 'radiant energy' *could* have produced the image. While traces of iron might be derived from blood or, for that matter from rouge or some other iron-containing pigment, other traces of mercury, also detected on certain parts of the shroud, could not have come from blood but could have been derived from the artist's pigment, vermilion.

While the scientific study of the shroud and the composition of the pigments on it, quite apart from the results of Bishop de Poitier's investigations carried out six hundred years earlier, imply that it was manufactured according to the recognized laws of nature, it runs counter to the cutting edge of Occam's razor to put forward another explanation – and a supernatural one, at that – of its origin, no matter how many authors write books about it or television presenters discuss it in their chat shows. That way lies fallacy.

SPOON BENDING

During the 1970s, a remarkable amount of attention was paid to the conjuring tricks performed by a quick-witted, handsome, plausible, former Israeli paratrooper called Uri Geller. The item in his repertoire which predominantly caught the public eye was his seeming ability to bend spoons, keys and other metal objects by what he claimed to be the unaided power of the human mind. There was nothing particularly unusual in these demonstrations which had long been the stock in trade of conjurers. What was remarkable, however, in the allegedly rational societies of Great Britain, the United States and other supposedly 'advanced' communities, was that a number of educated people who should have known better, including a few academic physicists, took Uri Geller's spoon bending seriously, thus confounding fallacy with reality.

Conjuring goes back to the days of antiquity. Not only did the priests and medicine men perform wonders which were believed by the faithful, but the effects achieved by conjurers whose only object was to entertain and amaze were believed by their simple-minded audiences to be due to the intervention of occult forces. It has been long understood, one would have imagined, that, as the cool words of an encyclopaedia put it, 'conjuring is the art of enter-taining by pretended performance of those things which cannot be done. The conjurer is an actor who, to perform his feats, combines psychology with manual dexterity.' This is understood, is it not? How dangerous then, is the phenomenon sparked off by Geller, inflamed by journalists and the hosts of television chat shows, accepted by a credulous generation unable to distinguish between the real technological 'marvels', which affect their lives one by one in quick succession, and fallacy.

Like other conjurers before him, Geller claimed that he performed his wonders – not only spoon bending but reproducing hidden drawings, starting stopped watches and deflecting magnetic compasses – by occult means. Furthermore, he was bold enough to submit himself to what the people who carried it out considered to be scientific investigation. The trouble was, however, that scientists are particularly unqualified to discover the devious procedures of conjurers. The quickness of the hand may not always deceive the eye, but the skilful patter of the magician and the movements of the right hand on which the eye is fixed will distract attention from what the left hand is doing. Geller does not always succeed under scrutiny with his metal bending. Then he may suddenly carry off a key to a nearby water tap, claiming to have found that running water helps the keys to bend under the influence of the occult forces he commands. Quite so. On the other hand, it is easier to apply ordinary mechanical force to a key if one end is stuck into the outlet of a water tap.

Dr John Taylor, a theoretical physicist from the University of London but a man who has also written about the effect of the astronomical phenomenon known as a 'black hole' on spiritualism, on Christianity and on dialectical materialism, took Geller's performances at their face value. He even went to the length of allowing members of a group of 11-year-old children who, it was alleged, possessed the occult power of spoon bending, to go out of sight or even to go home when inducing their ironmongery to bend since 'this feature of bending not happening when the object is being watched – "the shyness factor" – is very common'. I bet it is! But although the more credulous Dr Taylor was prepared to accept as truth the occult effects wrought by the children recruited by Geller during a television programme, a more sceptical group of scientists from the University of Bath – possibly with 11-year-old children of their own – organized a more rigorous test. The small innocent adepts were set to work to get their spoons to bend. The observer present in the room with them did not see anyone cheating. However, the scientists had taken the precaution of making provision for several other observers who watched what was going on from outside the room through one-way mirrors. Of the six children purported to possess supernatural powers over metal, five were seen to cheat when the attention of the observer in the room was distracted. They then hurriedly bent their spoons by hand or over the top of the table or across the edge of a chair. The spoon belonging to the sixth child, who was not seen to cheat, did not get bent.

Educated and sophisticated people who go to see a conjurer do not expect to detect how the tricks are done. And throughout history there have arisen from time to time particularly talented magicians who understand, either by careful thought and study or by natural talent, how to deceive their audiences. Yet sensible modern audiences know perfectly well that what they are seeing is a trick.

It was Einstein who wrote: '*Raffiniert ist der Herr Gott, aber Boshaft ist Er nicht*' (the Creator is subtle, but he is not mischievous). Scientists base their studies on the assumption that there is regularity in the universe if they only possess the talent to unravel its subtlety. Conjurers, on the other hand, set out to be mischievous and to deceive. Their motto is 'never give a sucker a break'. It behoves us, if we hope to live a sensible life, whether we are scientists or merely ordinary citizens, not to be suckers.

STARVING MILLIONS

There are large numbers of kindly people who read the newspapers, listen to the radio and watch serious documentary programmes on the television who have become convinced that half the world's population is starving. This is a fallacy. It is true that there are people, particularly in certain tropical countries, who live in conditions of extreme poverty. These have been calculated to amount to about 2 per cent of the human race. This proportion, although very different from the 50 per cent which has been bruited about, nevertheless comprises some forty starving millions. Deplorable though this may appear to all humane men and women who feel concern for their fellow creatures, it is not at all clear whether this proportion is greater or, as is more likely, less than it has been throughout history.

Before people talk about starvation, they should know what it is they are talking about. Men and women may live in tolerable health for the whole of their lives on what those of us whose standard of life is higher would consider to be half rations. Such a state of affairs existed in Ireland when the nineteenth century began. When, however, in 1846, 1847 and 1848, potato blight destroyed completely the crops of potatoes which served the Irish people as their main article of diet, then it could in deadly truth be claimed that millions of the population starved and many died. Bad though things may be in the pictures selected by the welfare people to excite our sympathy for an impoverished community, they scarcely represent starvation.

Starvation and famine have traditionally been recognized as concomitants of war. In medieval times, the besieging army surrounding a city knew that their main military instrument was more likely to be the starvation of the citizens, their wives and their children, grandfathers and grandmothers, than the overthrow of the opposing garrison by the potency of their artillery. The same principle was used in the siege of Paris in the Franco–German war of the last century, as in the siege of Leningrad in World War II of this century. Even following the armistice purporting to end World War I in 1918, the Allies continued the blockade of Germany and the Central Powers for a full year more so that the rigours of starvation here and there should render Germany more amenable to the final terms of surrender.

Wars, although regrettably frequent, are hardly a continuous state of affairs for most people nor, when the phrase 'the starving millions' is used, are the consequences of battle usually implied. The common assumption is that people starve because there is not enough food in the world to go round or, in some people's view, because the world cannot produce enough food. The statistics show that this is a fallacy. During the three decades or more since the Food and Agriculture Organization of the United Nations have been collecting figures as best they can of the world's food supply, the amount of food produced has consistently been increasing at a rate faster than has the number of mouths to eat it. And not only has the food supply for the whole world been increasing somewhat faster than the world's population, but so has the amount of food grown in the so-called 'developing' countries increased faster than their populations. Most remarkable of all is that India, a country where from time to time throughout history when the monsoon fails there have been famines in which people starved in badly hit parts of the land, in the 1980s became a *grain exporting* nation.

The application of science to agriculture has probably been more productive than its application to any other area of human endeavour. Yields of wheat, rice and maize have been multiplied within our own lifetimes and the production of meat, milk and eggs has been increased in parallel. People suffer hardship and some of them starve, not because there is no food for them to eat, but because they have no money to buy it, because they are involved in war, or because their community is inefficiently or corruptly run. But starvation does not involve half the human race or, indeed, in many instances, starving *millions*.

One of the reasons why the fallacy of starving millions gained currency arose from the writings of that remarkable scientist and first Director General of the Food and Agriculture Organization of the UN, Sir John – later Lord – Boyd Orr. In his book, *Food, Health and Income*, published in 1936, he compared the composition, in terms of calories, protein, minerals and vitamins, of the diet eaten by members of British families living on different incomes with estimates of what the composition of a perfect diet should be. Although none of the families were starving, not even the poorest, the poorer they were the more often the consumption of one or other of the vitamins or minerals, and sometimes even of the calories, failed to come up to the estimated figures for perfection. It did not take long for those concerned with the welfare of others, not only of poor British families but also with the families of all the people on earth, to bracket anyone whose diet could be estimated to contain less than it should of vitamin C or calcium or whatever it might be with the 'starving millions'. Only later did it emerge that some of the estimates of a perfect diet were too high. And it was also realized that malnutrition or even undernutrition, though possibly undesirable, could be very far from starvation. For example, thirty years ago it was assumed that the Japanese were a small race:

certainly effective, but small. It was then observed that Japanese whose parents had emigrated to Hawaii and who had been brought up on American food, grew taller and generally bigger than did their cousins who had stayed behind in Japan. The point to remember is that there is a wide difference between optimum nutrition, acceptable nutrition (to Japanese in Japan, for example) and malnutrition – and starvation. Clearly, therefore, it is important to understand quite precisely what one is talking about in order to avoid the fallacy of believing in more starving millions than there really are. The Japanese would hardly have been gratified had they been included among the starving just after they had defeated the Russians in 1905 or sunk the American fleet at Pearl Harbour in 1941.

#

THIRTEEN

Sensible people know that luck is an important factor in many of the various aspects of life. Mathematicians and scientists can calculate with considerable precision the degree to which luck – under the title of chance or probability – comes into their equations. Insurance companies dispose with prudence of the large sums of

money they handle providing they understand the influence of luck in human affairs. A conscientious government will do what it can to prevent its citizens dying through smoking cigarettes on the one hand, or being killed in road accidents on the other. The basis for the government's action is the statistical probability of people being killed by tobacco smoke or motor smashes. But whether it is you or whether it is I who is killed by lung cancer or careless driving is a matter of luck. A friend of mine, after being held up for ten minutes on the motorway under a road bridge, got out of his car to find out the cause of the stoppage. He discovered that both ahead of him and behind there had been multiple pile-ups, smashed cars and bodies lying on the road. The fact that he and his car were untouched was a matter of luck.

Any rational citizen is well aware that luck is a serious matter. It is, therefore, foolish to believe – or even to half-believe – in fallacy about luck, as, indeed, about anything else. Such a fallacy is the widely accepted belief that thirteen is an unlucky number. So ridiculous is this fallacy that in France municipalities do not use thirteen in numbering houses in a street. There are also agencies prepared to supply a fourteenth guest to dinner parties which would otherwise comprise thirteen people. In Italy, there is never a ticket numbered thirteen in any national lottery, while in the United States, when skyscrapers are being built, there may be storeys from 1 to 12 and from 14 to 40, but no 13.

The fallacy about 13 goes back before the Christian era. An early mention occurs in Norse mythology. Twelve gods invited to a banquet in Valhalla had their peace destroyed by the arrival un-invited of Loki, the spirit of strife. It was later that the thirteen at the Last Supper reinforced the notion that this number of itself was unlucky.

TOBACCO

Since tobacco was first introduced into Europe in the sixteenth century, it has been involved in all sorts of fallacies. Even today, when the understanding of the consequences of at least one of its uses, namely cigarette smoking, has been clarified, fallacy has not entirely come to an end.

When tobacco first came into use in Spain and Portugal and, shortly afterwards, in Belgium, France and England, it was considered to be a universal remedy and – largely because it was new and derived from the lore of the mysterious American Indians – was warmly recommended by physicians. The American Indians used it in magical rites. The smoke coming out of a man's mouth was part of his very spirit. The carved pipes from which it was smoked were sacred objects to be used for specified purposes. There was one pipe with its associated ceremony to be used for war and another for peace. Evil spirits could be appeased by the incense of tobacco smoke. In Brazil, sixteenth-century travellers found the men smoking what amounted to over-sized cigars made of tobacco so strong that it could render them unconscious, carried away, as it were, into a spirit world. In the island of Hispaniola, the sniffing of tobacco smoke was done through hollow sticks and continued until the sniffer lost his senses. This practice was considered to be not only very healthy but very holy as well.

In Europe, tobacco fallacies quickly burgeoned. Tobacco was claimed to be a remedy for ulcers, both benign and cancerous. The smoke was accepted as relieving asthma, headaches, consumption, syphilis, the falling sickness (epilepsy) and dropsy, while preparations made from tobacco leaves were believed to cure ringworm, scabies, rheumatism, toothache and 'venomous' wounds. The most remarkable use of tobacco smoke, based on its presumed therapeutic benefits was as a clyster, that is to say as an enema, for the administration of which a special instrument was designed in the seventeenth century. 'The smoke so applied', a contemporary physician wrote, 'is at once an evacutory, counter-irritant, diuretic, anodyne or sedative and the warm air has a beneficial effect as well'. It is indeed remarkable what people can believe if they try.

But a new scene was dawning. The largely fallacious claims on behalf of tobacco were being overtaken by equally fallacious claims for its harmfulness. The attacks on tobacco probably began on moral rather than on scientific grounds and were led by the medical profession who, in the seventeenth century just as today, hated to see what they considered to be serious medical remedies used for fun. King James I was in the forefront of the battle, stimulated, it was said, by his personal dislike of Sir Walter Raleigh, who was credited with introducing tobacco into England. The king's book entitled *A Counterblast to Tobacco*, after asserting that the benefits attributed to tobacco were unjustified, claiming that, on the contrary, many people smoked themselves to death, and asserting that 'this wild custom is a form of sinful and shameful lust, a kind of drunkenness', winds up with the denunciation that smoking is 'a custom loathsome to the eye, hateful to the nose, harmful to the braine, dangerous to the lungs, and in the blacke stinking fume thereof, neerest resembling the horrible Stigian smoke of the pit that is bottomless'. If only the government today printed prose like that on cigarette packets they really could expect results!

The belief in tobacco as a remedy for almost all human ills persisted well into the eighteenth century. At that time the use of tobacco was widespread, in the form of snuff as well as for smoking in cigars or pipes, which were particularly popular in England and France. Cigarettes only came into popular favour in the nineteenth century. Gradually, however, attacks on tobacco increased and anti-smoking societies appeared, chiefly in England, France and the United States. A typical nineteenth-century rhyme ran:

> Tobacco is a nasty weed,
> It emp's the pockets,
> Spoils the clothes
> And makes a chimney of the nose.

Only in our own times and after prolonged trials, of which the results were subjected to statistical analysis, can it be seen that the wild fallacies, both in favour of tobacco and against it, were equally unsound and it has become clear that cigarette smoking (let us say nothing about snuff, cigars or pipes until we're sure) can be linked with heart disease and cancer of the lung.

U

UFOs

In early and biblical times, when it was believed deeply that a celestial city crowded with the heavenly host was to be found above in the sky – not, as we now know, a swarm of mechanical satellites and, further out, a multitude of 'black holes' – many people claimed to have seen angels. These were of various types. Isaiah, for example, reported that the seraphim were like men but possessed six wings. Ezekiel described the cherubim as being similar to people but with four wings and four faces. There were those who could vouch that they had seen Old Nick, the devil, a fallen angel, with horns and a tail.

In our modern technological age, angels have fallen out of the public consciousness just as did the classical gods and goddesses before them, who were once seen driving their chariots across the sky. Instead, dazzled by the remarkable achievements of cosmic rocketry which, although it is firmly based on the entirely understandable principles of engineering and astronomy, is not understood by ordinary people, certain members of the public began to see 'flying saucers' and unidentified flying objects (UFOs) – supernatural but satisfyingly familiar things. The sightings first began to be reported in numbers up to thirty years ago in the United States where the citizens have, beyond all others, the most devout faith in higher technology. So numerous and so detailed were the reports of UFOs that the United States Air Force negotiated with the University of Colorado to set up a high-powered scientific committee to investigate the matter. This the committee did with enormous thoroughness, even to the extent of interviewing 'a most articulate gentleman [who] told . . . with calm good manners . . . [and in] some detail about how his wife's grandfather immigrated to the United States from the *Andromeda nebula*'. He brought a piece of celestial foil with him, which his wife's grandfather had, he said, brought down from the stars to substantiate his story. Unluckily, the committee identified the foil as a particular alloy

1145, treated with a special lacquer, Keratyn, manufactured in Brooklyn, New York.

The committee studied some sixty reports of seemingly unusual happenings but found no evidence to support the suggestion of any of them being due to people or things originating in outer space. Of 35 incidents supported by photographic evidence, one-quarter of the photographs or films had obviously been faked, a second quarter were of natural phenomena which had been wrongly identified, and a third quarter gave so little information as to be quite useless. Of the rest, most were accompanied by too little supporting evidence to allow any conclusion to be drawn at all. Only two pieces of film were inexplicable to the expert committee. The number of possible natural explanations, according to the committee, for saucers seen moving across the sky and 'blips' appearing on radar screens was prodigious. The physics of such optical and electronic phenomena is complex. Ball lightning and meteorites warrant a study to themselves, while the number of high-altitude weather balloons drifting around in the upper atmosphere came as something of a surprise to the UFO investigators.

And always, there were the tall stories and the people who were prepared to believe them. What is to be done with the two shipyard workers in Pascagoula who, in 1973, reported that they had been taken aboard a flying saucer to be interrogated by spacemen hostile to the United States? As soon as these shipyard workers announced their reappearance on earth, back at Pascagoula, they were famous. Within forty-eight hours they were television personalities with their own booking agent. Interviews with them, during which they gave vivid accounts of the lobster-clawed creatures from outer space who had abducted them, were reported worldwide by the newspapers. Two professors from reputable universities discussed their adventures respectfully. It should perhaps be noted that the subjects in which these academics were expert were astronomy and engineering, not law, which is a discipline in which people are trained to assess the reliability of witnesses. Would it be unkind to suggest that there are people, some of whom are professors but most of whom are not, who do believe stories such as that told by the men from Pascagoula and indeed, when they *want* to believe, will believe anything?

The wise scientific committee from the University of Colorado did a splendid job in painstakingly considering every account of UFO sightings and showing how each could be attributed to natural events (among which it is sad to have to include lying and cheating). The crew of an army helicopter in Ohio were seriously frightened by what they took to be a near miss by a very bright UFO which shone, first reddish, then green, then white, moving towards them, they thought, at high speed. The pilot took diversionary action at the time and later told his story on the inevitable television talk show. The crew collected $5000 as a prize for the 'best UFO case of 1973'. Later on, after the evidence had been carefully sifted, sceptical investigators of the incident concluded that a distant meteorite viewed through the green tinted upper canopy of the aircraft, through the clear windscreen, and dimming red in the distance constituted a more plausible explanation of what the airmen had really seen.

The scientific study of unidentified flying objects was useful on three counts. First, it calmed the public alarm which was sweeping the United States; second, it illustrated the care which needs to be taken by scientists in assessing the evidence they study before, ever so tentatively, they draw conclusions from it; and, thirdly, they concluded that 'further extensive study of UFOs probably cannot be justified in the expectation that science will be advanced thereby'. It is, after all, more sensible for people to bring their minds to bear on what promises to be a real problem rather than dissipate their energies on what looks like – and often turns out to be – a fallacy.

As was to be expected, the UFOlogists and those who perversely continue to believe in their mysteriousness, who write books about UFOs and who accuse the American CIA of having mounted a 'cosmic Watergate' cover-up, continue in their beliefs. But as time goes on and sensible people become more practised in identifying false and spurious evidence, the lack of real, solid evidence itself gives added strength to the conclusion that men from outer space and their flying saucers need cause us no alarm – because they are a fallacy and do not exist.

★

WARTS

Until comparatively recently, when warts, or *papillomas*, as they are now called, were found to be due to papillomaviruses, they were rather mysterious things. A wart is, of course, as defined in the dictionary, 'a small, round, dry, tough excrescence on the skin, especially common on the hands of young persons'. The medical profession, as long ago as 1552, called it a *condyloma*. In fact no one knows very much about warts, what causes them and, more important, what makes them disappear quite suddenly. Here lies the origin of the fallacies which have grown up about them. The fallacies themselves, it could be said, are not particularly dangerous, in view of the fact that warts are not particularly important, although a nuisance and mildly disfiguring. Much more important and damaging, in my view, is the *belief* in the fallacies about the cause of warts and the variety of bizarre cures which have been proposed, which are not cures at all because most warts in the end disappear on their own.

An example of the way in which comparatively harmless warts have led to harmful belief in the unbelievable is the identification by what one would hope to be otherwise sensible people of a particular species of grasshopper, *Gryllus verrucivorus*, as a 'wart biter' – or, in German, a *warzenbeisser* – supposed to destroy warts by biting them off. This is a piece of magic left over from a more credulous age. Magic is a system widely current in primitive and superstitious cultures but which, it could have been hoped, had died away in more civilized societies. Magic depends on spells and ritual and on people irrational enough to believe in their efficacy. Magic may be complex and systematized and give the impression of being a science. This, however, it is not. Sir James Frazer described it as 'bastard science' because, unlike science, it does not depend on viewing things as they are in the real universe but on the way its practitioners would like things to be. Sprinkling water on the ground, chanting certain spells and dancing certain dances do not bring rain, even if it may

sometimes rain after these things have been done. Nor does spitting on a wart and going to bed on the night of the new moon with it encircled by a hair, both of which have been recommended, make it disappear.

John Wesley collected a number of useful procedures for healing the sick during the course of his diverse missions. But in spite of his good intentions and the sincerity of his preaching, his prescription that rubbing a wart every day with a radish or with the juice of a marigold did not influence the length of time it remained on a boy's finger. Mankind has throughout its history wanted to be able to exercise power over its surroundings. For most of this history, men did not, in fact, understand how to influence the harsh strokes of circumstance. Lacking real power, they invented bogus rituals of magic. A parent, watching his child dying of consumption, could be forgiven for indulging in prayers for the sick, or for the purchase of an amulet from a sorcerer. Today, through the use of reason, streptomycin has become available by which the dread disease of consumption – that is tuberculosis – has ceased to be a scourge to humanity. But while our reason allows us to cope with ills before which we were once helpless, there are circumstances with which we still cannot cope. When these arise, it is good to recognize our own helplessness rather than pretend that a fallacy is the truth. Yet even though we do not know why a schoolboy's fingers are covered with warts, we do know that when he grows up they will probably cure themselves.

WELSH RABBIT

There are two fallacies entangled in Welsh Rabbit. The first is that it is not a rabbit at all. The fact that an agreeable, if simple, concoction of melted cheese poured over a slice of buttered toast was, in 1725 or thereabouts, called a 'Welsh rabbit' is a minor example of what we should today describe as racism. In the eighteenth century (let us make no comment about times before or since) the English looked down on the Welsh. They derided their poverty and cast doubts on their honesty. They even made fun of them for having no rabbits in Wales, forgetting – if, indeed, they had ever known it – that rabbits were not native to England but were introduced from the Iberian Peninsular in the twelfth century. It was put about that to pretend that they were eating meat, the Welsh were compelled to deceive themselves with bread and cheese. As the English rhyme had it:

Jenny ap-Rice hur could eat nothing nice,
A dainty Welsh rabbit? – go toast her a slice
Of cheese if you please, which better agrees
With the tooth of poor Taffy than physic and fees.
A pound Jenny got, and brought to his cot
A prime double Gloucester, all hot, piping hot –
Which being a bunny without any bones
Was custard and mustard to Taffy ap-Jones.

This is the straightforward part of the fallacy in which, for a perfectly good, if not altogether creditable, reason, a dish primarily made of cheese was called 'rabbit'. But then, in 1785, the English *literati*, having become genteel with the passage of time and, perhaps, feeling some slight sense of shame at having been disparaging to the Welsh, pretended that they had never been any such thing, that 'rabbit' was a corruption of 'rare bit' and that it was clever of the Welsh to have thought up such a comestible.

Personally, I prefer the first version.

WORMWOOD

Wormwood has nothing to do with either worms or wood. It is a fairly common plant which grows on waste ground in Great Britain. It is also to be found in other parts of Europe and in America as well. Its proper name is *Artemesia absinthia*. It has a characteristic bitter taste. At one time it was used in medicines and for flavouring what was always recognized to be the highly toxic alcoholic beverage, absinth, popular in France and Switzerland. In its traditional form, the best that can be said for absinth is that it quickly intoxicates those who drink it. The wormwood is reputed to act powerfully on the nerve centres, and to cause delirium, followed, in the case of particularly persistent drinkers, by idiocy.

YETI

There is a long-established Tibetan legend among the people who live near the high mountains that there is a mysterious creature, the yeti, that stalks about in the snow. This creature, unknown to nature or to science, is called the *metoh kangmi*, translated – perhaps unfortunately – into English as 'abominable snowman'. The obstacle preventing universal belief in the existence of this creature is that no one has ever seen it. While it remains in this state, it is, I feel, justifiable to regard it as a fallacy.

The only evidence for the existence of the yeti seems to be occasional traces of its footprints in the snow. But although several people have seen these footprints, there is little unanimity about the animal that could have produced them. There are those who believe that the footprints are those of a grey wolf; others favour the snow leopard; while the Himalayan langur has its supporters too. Perhaps the front runner of the whole pack of candidates is the red bear. That the tracks are his has the support of George Cansdale of the London Zoo. Among all these *possibles*, it is reasonable to accept meanwhile that the yeti, the abominable snowman, might be left meanwhile as an *impossible* – a fallacy.

EPILOGUE

Fallacies come in all sizes, big and important as well as small and trivial, and are of various sorts. There are those that arise out of ignorance. Little harm, one might argue, comes from mistaking the nature of Bombay duck or the bristles in a camel's hair brush. Yet knowledge is delightful, whether it is directly useful or not; this underlies the delights of scientific research. Knowledge, too, protects the citizen against the insidious damage of the trickster and the charlatan who, from malice or the pursuit of money, artfully construct fallacies to deceive the more gullible of their fellows. Piltdown Man deceived a generation of unsuspecting searchers after the truth, while spoon-bending, a harmless trick when used to entertain, allowed mischievous trickery to exert a damaging effect on the minds of ordinary people and some scientists as well.

Fallacies are perhaps most damaging of all when they cause sincere people to deceive themselves. It is bad enough for the misguided inventor to waste his life and spend his fortune in a vain attempt to build a perpetual-motion machine. In many ways it is worse for the disciples of a fallacious doctrine – astrology, perhaps, or the belief that there are hostile little men from outer space preparing to take over the city and then the world – who live in fear and dare not take any action pending the receipt of a favourable omen.

I have discussed only a bare 64 fallacies, some based on ignorance, others on trickery, and others again on self-deception and gullibility, but there are many more. It is distressing to observe how many current fallacies there are, each with a following of credulous disciples. The ponderous works of Immanuel Valikovski, postulating there having been a comet in 1500 BC ejected by Jupiter, twice passing close to the earth, once close to Mars, until in 700 BC it was transformed into the planet Venus, have believers on both sides of the Atlantic. These citizens of today's world, familiar with communication satellites and space shuttles, dependent as they are on Newton's Laws, are thus seen to embrace an absurd fable which ignores the hard-won understanding of the conservation of momentum, energy and mass, as well as the laws of gravity. Equally sad is the eagerness – in the New World as in the Old – of journalists, editors and producers to pander to the public appetite for believing in and shuddering at the unbelievable.

Believe me, dear public, and dear ladies and gentlemen of the media, truth is more delightful than fallacy. Copper bangles will *not* do your rheumatism any good, neither is your eyesight improved by wearing earrings pierced through the lobes of your ears; while soothsayers have been signally unsuccessful in forecasting the winner of the Derby. Neither can spoons be bent merely by taking thought. Thinking can be better employed in seriously striving to understand the real world.